General editor: Graham Handley

C000108234

Brodie's Notes on Jane Austen's

Pride and Prejudice

Graham Handley MA PhD

Formerly Principal Lecturer and Head of English Department, The College of All Saints, Tottenham

Pan Books London, Sydney and Auckland

First published 1986 by Pan Books Ltd
Cavaye Place, London SW10 9PG
9 8 7 6 5 4
© Pan Books Ltd 1986
ISBN 0 330 50208 5
Photoset by Parker Typesetting Service, Leicester
Printed and bound in Great Britain by
Richard Clay Ltd, Bungay, Suffolk

Contents

Page references in these Notes are to the Pan
edition of *Pride and Prejudice*, but references
are also given to particular chapters, so that
the Notes may be used with any edition of the novel.

Preface

The intention throughout this study aid is to stimulate and guide, to encourage the reader's *involvement* in the text, to develop disciplined critical responses and a sure understanding of the main details in the chosen text.

Brodie's Notes provide a summary of the plot of the play or novel followed by act, scene or chapter summaries each of which will have an accompanying critical commentary designed to underline the most important literary and factual details. Textual notes will be explanatory or critical (sometimes both), defining what is difficult or obscure on the one hand, or stressing points of character, style or plot on the other. Revision questions will be set on each act or group of chapters to test the student's careful application to the text of the prescribed book.

The second section of each of these study aids will consist of a critical examination of the author's art. This will cover such major elements as characterization, style, structure, setting, theme(s) or any other aspect of the book which the editor considers needs close study. The paramount aim is to send the student back to the text. Each study aid will include a series of general questions which require a detailed knowledge of the set book; the first of these questions will have notes by the editor of what *might* be included in a written answer. A short list of books considered useful as background reading for the student will be provided at the end.

Graham Handley

The author and her work

Jane Austen was born in December 1775 at Steventon in Hampshire where her father George Austen was the Rector; here she spent her childhood and young womanhood, with occasional trips away from home. Her father, who was later to recognize his daughter's great talents, took pupils and prepared them for Oxford, where two of his sons studied. Her mother was a keen gardener, had a good sense of humour, but suffered from lengthy bouts of ill-health. The Austens were a close family. The eldest son James had a curacy, and later succeeded his father at Steventon; while still a boy the next brother Edward was adopted and brought up by well-to-do cousins in Kent. Henry, next in age, was close to Jane sympathetically, sharing her sense of humour and the quality of her wit. Closest of all was her sister Cassandra, to whom many of Jane's letters were written and with whom she shared strong bonds of interest and affection. Cassandra once told her sister – perhaps with a shade of mockery – 'You are indeed the finest comic writer of the present age.' Jane's two other brothers, Charles and Frank, entered the Navy, both achieving high rank.

Jane was encouraged to write, her father even corresponding with a publisher on her account, and often she read aloud her early burlesques. Their father's sister, who married a Frenchman, later became strongly attached to the Austens at Steventon. Her husband was executed in 1794 at the height of the French revolutionary excesses, and it was probably in part through her that Jane learnt much of the world outside Steventon.

There is little doubt that Jane Austen's style was influenced by the great writers of the 18th century, and in her impressionable years she was certainly reading Dr Johnson, Goldsmith, Crabbe, Cowper, and many travel writers. She read novels too, writing burlesques and parodies of some of her contemporaries. Before she was sixteen she had written much, and her juvenilia have been published as *Volume the First*, the *Second* and *Third*, each with editorial commentaries. The second volume is *Love and Freindship* (*sic*), in part written in the form of letters, the epistolary style which she inherited from the great 18th century novelist Samuel Richardson. There is some evidence that *Elinor and Marianne* (later *Sense and Sensibility*) was at first written in the epistolary mode before it was later revised. *First Impressions* (later to become *Pride and Prejudice*) was finished in 1797 and offered by Mr Austen to the London publisher Cadell, who turned it down. By 1798 Jane was well on with *Susan*, later to be turned into *Northanger Abbey*, her satire on the Gothic novel.

Mr and Mrs Austen were bent on retiring to Bath, and the family settled there shortly after the turn of the century. Jane never really liked Bath and is thought to have had an unhappy love affair shortly after the move. However, by 1803 she had revised the early version of *Northanger Abbey* and the manuscript was accepted by the London publisher Crosby though it remained unpublished.

In 1804 Jane Austen's great friend Mrs Lefroy died, and in the following year she lost her father. Outside her family, she had received no recognition yet as an authoress. In 1807 the family moved to Southampton, where they were to stay for three years. They became close to Edward at Godmersham, and when his wife died leaving seven children, Jane and Cassandra found themselves often occupied as aunts to this tribe of nephews and nieces.

The next move was to Chawton in Hampshire, where she was generally happy. *Sense and Sensibility* was published in 1811, and in 1813 *Pride and Prejudice* appeared. As Jane wrote to Cassandra, 'I have got my own darling child from London.' She has left on record how much she loved her leading character, Elizabeth Bennet. Jane wrote, as we know, in the sitting-room, revising and proof-reading as well as drafting her work. What she wrote was published anonymously, and we know from the evidence of her brother Henry that she took great care to get everything just right before letting the final copy go to the printer.

Mansfield Park appeared in 1814, *Emma* in 1815, the latter invoking a very generous review from Sir Walter Scott and an authority from the Prince Regent's librarian J. S. Clarke granting the author permission to dedicate any future work to the Prince Regent. He even went on to suggest that she might like to write 'an historical romance, illustrative of the august history of the House of Coburg'. But her horizons, though narrower in terms of historical compass, were perhaps wider in terms of the exploration of the human heart. Henry got back the copyright of *Northanger Abbey*, and in 1816 Jane drafted the Advertisement for the novel, which was later printed posthumously with the text. But she had another novel on her hands, having begun *Persuasion*; she finished it in July 1816, though she cancelled one chapter which was virtually completely re-drafted. This novel and *Northanger Abbey* were put aside and work on *Sanditon* was begun early in 1817. By March of that year she was very ill; in May she went with Cassandra to Winchester, where she received good medical attention. It was of no avail, and on 18 July Jane died, leaving *Northanger Abbey* and *Persuasion* to be published in 1818.

Thus lived and died in unremarkable and retired obscurity one of the greatest English novelists. Throughout her writings her moral stance is clear, uncompromising in its perspective, never complacent or smug. She gave the English novel increased and serious status, thus preparing the way for the great writers of the nineteenth century. It has been said that her canvas was narrow, and there is no doubt that she would have acknowledged this. Such great events of her time as the French Revolution and the ensuing wars, excesses, idealisms and struggles, find no place in her work. But her range encompassed the novelist's material, the affairs of the human heart; and with refinements of style and a meticulous observation of character in action and interaction, she brought to fictional characters a closer and deeper scrutiny than they had hitherto received.

Jane Austen learned much from those who had written before her, but she imposed her own compactness of form, giving to her characters a consistent psychology and development that was to influence not only the 19th century novelists but those who were to write from the consciousness of character in the 20th. Those who feel that her writings are the skilful but narrow work of an old maid should ask themselves if sexual passion has ever been depicted so strongly – not indulgently, not salaciously, not sensationally – as in the feelings of Darcy for Elizabeth Bennet. The conventions within which Jane lived and wrote demanded a certain code of conduct and the acceptance of what must remain unuttered or unseen. Yet her awareness encompasses it all, and we know she knows, and that she intends us to know, that the gloss of polite conversation cannot hide people's basic motives and impulses. Her way is to be ironic without being cruel, satirical without being complacent, wise without being pretentious and, above all, humane and understanding in her attitude towards the human condition. The purity and directness of her dialogue has stood the test of our own time.

Jane's spirit is in many ways a comic one, and we might here invoke Meredith's words, 'The laughter of Comedy is impersonal and of unrivalled politeness.' Her country house and parsonage and Bath society seem unaware of tragedy, but she shows us life as it is. She steers between the fictional extremes of vinegar and saccharine by the simple expedient of being true to her ear and her eye; they never let her down.

Plot, themes, chronology, settings

Plot

Mr Bennet and his wife have five daughters, and the plot of the novel embraces the two eldest daughters and a younger daughter Lydia. Mrs Bennet's avowed aim for her daughters is marriage, and an early opportunity arises for her with the news that a neighbouring country house is to be rented to a gentleman called Bingley.

After Bingley's arrival, Mr Bennet visits him, and the acquaintance between the families develops. Bingley has with him his sisters as well as a proud and seemingly haughty friend, Darcy. Bingley and Jane seem to be getting on well; Darcy is, despite himself, attracted to the second daughter, Elizabeth.

When Jane Bennet is taken ill while at Netherfield, Elizabeth goes to nurse her. There she finds herself much in the company of Darcy who, while not acknowledging it openly, finds himself falling in love with her.

Mr Collins, heir to the Bennet estate, writes to announce that he will be visiting the family. Meanwhile the younger daughters continue their pursuit of the local militia and so meet an officer named Wickham. Darcy meets Wickham in the company of the Misses Bennet, but each reacts coldly to the other. Wickham tells Elizabeth of how he has suffered in the past at the hands of Darcy. This serves to confirm Elizabeth's prejudice against Darcy.

Finding Jane probably spoken for, Mr Collins proposes to Elizabeth and, being turned down, quickly switches to her friend and neighbour, Charlotte Lucas, who accepts him. Elizabeth visits Hunsford Parsonage to see her old friend Charlotte and her new husband, and while there also visits Rosings Park from time to time to see Mr Collins' patroness – and Darcy's aunt – Lady Catherine de Bourgh. While Elizabeth is at Hunsford Darcy and another nephew of Lady Catherine's, Colonel Fitzwilliam, visit Lady Catherine. Elizabeth learns from Colonel Fitzwilliam that Darcy has recently helped Bingley to avoid an undesirable romantic attachment. Elizabeth is angered by this, but further shocked and angered when Darcy actually proposes to her in rather a condescending way. She scornfully rejects him, accusing him of coming between Bingley and Jane and of treating Wickham badly.

The next morning Darcy gives her a letter in which he puts his side of the Wickham story. He also points to the shortcomings of Elizabeth's own family. On reflection, she is forced to acknowledge the truth of this. On her return home, Elizabeth learns that Mr Bennet has agreed to Lydia travelling to Brighton with Colonel Forster and his wife. Elizabeth sets off with the Gardiners on a visit to Derbyshire, and they visit Darcy's home at Pemberley, thinking that the owner is absent. Darcy returns unexpectedly and, after some initial embarrassment, Darcy is most courteous to her and to the Gardiners. Elizabeth meets Darcy's sister Georgiana as well as Miss Bingley and Bingley himself, and Elizabeth finds herself acknowledging Darcy's good qualities.

Elizabeth hears from Jane that Lydia has eloped with Wickham and decides to return home. Eventually the couple are traced and on a triumphant return home, Lydia in an unguarded moment reveals that Darcy was at her wedding. Elizabeth later learns from her aunt Mrs Gardiner how much Darcy has done for Lydia and her family.

The Bingleys and Darcy return to Netherfield, and soon Bingley and Jane become engaged; Lady Catherine de Bourgh pays an unexpected visit to Elizabeth, accusing her of contriving to marry Darcy, who is already promised, she says, to her own daughter, Lady Anne. Elizabeth gives no undertaking that she will not marry Darcy. When they next meet, he tells her that his love for her is unchanged and she in return acknowledges that her feelings towards him have changed. They marry, as do Jane and Bingley, and both couples set up homes in Derbyshire. Mrs Bennet has succeeded in her wish of seeing three of her daughters married.

Themes

The themes of *Pride and Prejudice* are in part indicated in the title and in part by the discarded original title *First Impressions*. One theme involves the presentation of marriage – as in the case of Mr and Mrs Bennet and, to a lesser degree, that of Charlotte Lucas and Mr Collins – the underlying moral comment being that marriages must be based on love, respect, compatibility of feelings and interests. Mr and Mrs Bennet have grown away from each other; Mr Collins and Charlotte are married because Charlotte needs security and is prepared to waive love; Wickham and Lydia marry but with no hope or understanding of lasting happiness because of the essential superficiality of their characters. Against this is set the strongest moral theme of the novel – the education of the feelings and the emotions, seen primarily in the persons of Elizabeth and Darcy, who rise beyond their pride and their prejudice – and certainly their first impressions – placing right judgement, respect and love before all else. Bingley and Jane complement this, though their actual relationship is sketched so lightly that they are merely a moral mirror to the two main characters.

Other themes which are given considered stress are those of moral responsibility (seen in the Gardiners, Darcy), lack of such responsibility (seen in Mr Bennet, Mrs Bennet, Lydia), snobbery (Lady Catherine), artificiality and insensitivity (Miss Bingley), true worth and kindliness (Colonel Fitzwilliam), pompous and sycophantic (and anti-Christian) attitudes as reflected in the behaviour and standards of Mr Collins. Throughout the novel we are aware of the fact that there is a moral code – assuredly the author's – which acts as a yardstick for judgement and action. Jane Austen is a moral writer, and her themes are the themes of life – love, respect, compatibility, friendship and their obverse sides – greed, snobbery, self-advancement, dishonesty, lying, irresponsibility.

Chronology

This is merely a brief indication of the time-scale of *Pride and Prejudice* which has been so admirably charted by R. W. Chapman in his exemplary edition of the novel (Oxford, 1923). The early action belongs to November 1811, with Mr Collins's visit and proposal (late November), the Bingleys leaving Netherfield (about the same time), the Gardiners arriving for Christmas and then taking Jane to London (30 December). Elizabeth goes to Hunsford in March 1812, Darcy proposes to her in April, and she goes to town later that month. By the middle of July Elizabeth is on holiday in Derbyshire with the Gardiners where she meets Darcy; Lydia elopes at the beginning of August, and a week later Elizabeth is back home helping to deal with the crisis. Lydia and Wickham are married by the end of the month. Soon Elizabeth learns of Darcy's role in the marriage, and just after the middle of September Bingley and Darcy are at Netherfield. Bingley proposes to Jane towards the end of the month, Lady Catherine pays her abortive visit to Elizabeth early in October and Darcy proposes shortly after this. There is therefore a double wedding before Christmas.

I have included this brief section to indicate the *meticulous* attention that Jane Austen paid to detail. She was obviously getting her revision of *First Impressions* just right (it had been written much earlier) by giving an accurate updating. The action occupies just over a year, which makes the structural and dramatic focus all the more effective as Plot, themes, chronology, settings give way to reason and love.

Settings

The period is almost certainly 1811–12 (see the preceding section on *Chronology*) with Longbourn, visits to nearby Meryton, the visit to Hunsford in Kent and then, for Elizabeth, the holiday in Derbyshire and the meeting with Darcy at Pemberley. Jane stays in London with the Gardiners. These settings provide the background for an account of the lives of comfortably off people, though these are of varying degree. Longbourn is in Hertfordshire, the estate being worth about £2000 a year, Mr Bennet having settled some £5000 on his wife and daughters. Bingley is wealthy, stays at Netherfield in Hertfordshire, but also has a town house in London. Darcy too has a town house, though he lives at Pemberley, and has a large fortune; we learn that £30,000 is settled on his sister Georgiana, hence the interest of Wickham.

As will be seen from the above, there is a constant emphasis placed on money. Mrs Bennet *needs* to marry off her daughters and Bingley provides an initial opportunity for one of them. And indeed Netherfield and Pemberley in their separate ways represent wealth. Rosings has status and wealth – and the aristocratic connection – while Mr Gardiner, though in trade, is successful in money matters. The country life depicted around Longbourn is rather dull, enlivened as far as the younger daughters are concerned by the presence of the militia nearby.

Bingley's arrival brings with it the prospect of dinner parties and balls.

Mr Bennet is following accepted practice in calling on Bingley and thus establishing the climate in which visits can be exchanged. Girls were taught to be useful but not independent, and their accomplishments included music, singing and drawing. Hunting and shooting were the chief sports of the men, but we get the impression from *Pride and Prejudice* of a leisured society in which there is much time for news and gossip, for walking, escorting, shopping. There is a strong sense of insularity in this kind of world and, apart from the movement of the militia, little sense of outside events. The settings provide the foreground for the dramatic narrative, whether in the Park at Rosings where Elizabeth encounters Darcy on her walks, or in the shrubbery at Longbourn where she encounters the much more fearsome Lady Catherine.

Chapter summaries, critical comment, textual notes and revision questions

Chapter 1

Mrs Bennet, intent on getting one of her daughters married, announces to her husband that a wealthy young man has moved into the neighbourhood. He has taken Netherfield Park, a fine house, and Mrs Bennet tries to persuade her husband to call on him in order to further her plans.

Commentary

Notice the superb opening to the novel, with its ironic generalization, a kind of sly humour on the part of the author before she gets to the actual situation. There is a natural ease of dialogue, husband and wife being finely contrasted, Mrs Bennet all words, Mr Bennet a kind of retired cynicism, though note his own wit when he suggests that 'Bingley might like you the best of the party' (p.2). Already there is the hint of competition with the Lucases, and a masterly closing of the chapter which defines Mrs Bennet's motivation: 'The business of her life was to get her daughters married; its solace was visiting and news.' (p.3).

chaise and four Open horse-drawn carriage.
Michaelmas This is the festival of St Michael, held on 29 September, one of the English quarter days.
four or five thousand a year A fortune in those days, probably equivalent to more than £100,000 by today's values.
engage for i.e. more than I wish to entertain.
chuses The archaic spelling of 'chooses'.
quickness i.e. intelligence, intellect.
consideration Concern.
parts Abilities.
caprice Whimsical, unpredictable behaviour.
develope Describe.

Chapter 2

Mr Bennet calls on Mr Bingley, but delays revealing this to his wife and daughters. The social forms have been established, and

Mr Bingley can now call on them. Mrs Bennet is of course delighted.

Commentary

We have some insight into the 'caprice' of Mr Bennet, shown in his secret visit to Mr Bingley. He begins by teasing his family, and we note the irritability of Mrs Bennet who fears that Mrs Long will have her nieces meet Mr Bingley in time to forestall her. Note the natural family atmosphere, with Mr Bennet in command of the situation, and even waxing satirically about the supposed 'deep reflection' of his dull daughter, Mary. His irony also embraces Kitty, he enjoys his production of the unexpected, while Mrs Bennet changes her mood to one of exultation and Lydia reveals her boldness.

trimming Adorning, decorating.
assemblies Social gatherings.
circumspection i.e. sense of propriety, what is socially correct.
the office i.e. of introduction.
tumult of joy Note the excessive feeling, which of course underlines
  Mrs Bennet's shallowness.

Chapter 3

After a few days Mr Bingley returns Mr Bennet's call, does not see the girls, and declines an invitation to dinner since he has to go to town. He soon returns to Longbourn, bringing with him his two sisters, his brother-in-law Mr Hurst and a striking friend, Mr Darcy. Bingley makes himself very agreeable when he attends a ball with his party, but Darcy proves stand-offish and disdainful. When she gets home Mrs Bennet, to her husband's impatience, gives him a loquacious account of the evening.

Commentary

Fine insight into the character of Mrs Bennet, with her hopes and fears re Bingley, and some set-piece description of Bingley and Darcy, the pride of the latter being stressed. Notice the focus on money (the fact that Darcy has £10,000 a year) and the deliberate contrast between Darcy and Bingley. Jane Austen is adept at capturing social and gossip reaction, hence the feeling against Darcy because of his manners. Elizabeth hears his comparative disparagement of her, but we note her spirit in telling the story against herself and her 'lively, playful disposition' (p.7). Nevertheless her 'first impressions' are unfavourable. We further note Mrs Bennet's stream of words which indicate the superficiality of her mind; in view of the end of the novel there is a very deliberate irony in Mrs Bennet's appraisal of Darcy as 'a most disagreeable, horrid man, not at all worth pleasing' (p.9).

intelligence Report.
mien Bearing, appearance.
decided i.e. pronounced upon.
fastidious Disdainful, choosy.
distinguished i.e. singled out for conversation.
event Result.
Miss King Note that this heiress is later pursued by Wickham.
Boulanger Country dance.
set downs i.e. put him down by sarcastic comment.

Chapter 4

Jane, the eldest daughter of the Bennets, discusses Bingley with her sister Elizabeth. They agree that Bingley is a very agreeable young man and Jane, who habitually thinks the best of people, rather likes his sisters too, but here Elizabeth has her reservations. A parallel discussion takes place of the Meryton assembly at Netherfield; Bingley praises Jane and his sisters agree with him, but Darcy, who is difficult to please, allows her to be pretty but thinks that she smiles too much.

Commentary

Jane is shown to be somewhat naive, Elizabeth ironic and witty in her comments. Already we see the mark of her independence, and her insight into Bingley's sisters is based on her common sense and breeding. The authorial irony reinforces Elizabeth's, for she notes that the sisters 'were therefore in every respect entitled to think well of themselves, and meanly of others' (p.10). The fact that their own fortune had been 'acquired by trade' (p.10) reinforces their inverted snobbery. The characters of

Bingley and Darcy are contrasted (contrast is at the heart of Jane Austen's narrative method); Bingley is impressionable, Darcy proud and contemptuous of what he has seen.

Affectation of candour i.e. pretend to see good in everyone.
pliancy of temper Yielding disposition.
seminaries i.e. schools, educational establishments.
the liberty of a manor i.e. the shooting rights which go with the property Bingley has rented.
to purchase i.e. buy the property outright.
of age i.e. twenty-one years old.
opposition Contrast.
ductility of his temper Sweetness of his nature.
understanding Intelligence.
allowed it to be so Agreed with what he said.

Chapter 5

Sir William Lucas and his family, neighbours of the Bennets, visit them after the Meryton assembly and they discuss the ball. All realize, to the delight of Mrs Bennet, that Bingley has distinguished Jane by his attentions; they agree that Darcy is proud, but Charlotte Lucas offers some defence of him on the grounds that he has a right to be proud. Mary Bennet, who prides herself on her 'reflections', treats the audience to a discourse on pride and vanity.

Commentary

The authorial irony is now deployed at the expense of Sir William Lucas, a harmless man but concerned with 'the pleasure of his own importance' (p.12). Charlotte is described as 'a sensible, intelligent young woman' (p.12), and again we note the accurate recording of dialogue, the incidence of overhearing (which plays a great part in the novel) and the social vulgarity and prejudice of Mrs Bennet. Elizabeth proves herself mistress of the antithetically witty remark at Darcy's expense – 'I could easily forgive *his* pride, if he had not mortified *mine*' (p.13). Mary reinforces our idea that she is pompous and dull.

an address An official welcome (here in his capacity of mayor).
disgust Dislike, shame.

St James's i.e. the court, the palace at Pall Mall, London, the home of British rulers from 1697 to 1837.

spoke to . . . ate up These are now archaic, being replaced by the correct 'spoken to' and 'eaten up'.

hack chaise Hired carriage.

Chapter 6

The Longbourn ladies visit Netherfield and their visit is returned. Charlotte and Elizabeth discuss Jane's feelings for Bingley, Charlotte advocating that she should use more encouragement, Elizabeth defining her sister's somewhat cautious nature. Darcy meanwhile is becoming very interested in Elizabeth (unknown to her) and listens to Elizabeth's conversation when they are at a gathering at Sir William Lucas's house. Elizabeth is not slow to make him aware of the fact that she knows this and, after she has sung and Mary has followed her by singing too, Sir William Lucas engages Darcy in conversation. Elizabeth refuses to dance with Darcy, but this makes her more intriguing to him. Indeed when Miss Bingley, who obviously has designs on him herself, speaks with amazement of his praise of Elizabeth, he listens to her 'with perfect indifference' (p.19).

Commentary

Elizabeth's keen-sightedness makes her note Mrs Hurst's and Miss Bingley's superciliousness, but she also has the sensitivity to be aware of Jane's composure and discretion, though she detects her sister's growing love for Bingley. Charlotte's advice that Jane should reveal that preference is an unashamed anticipation of her own reception later of Mr Collins. There is irony in the fact that Charlotte is right – Bingley does not know Jane's disposition and, influenced by Darcy, cannot know that he may injure her feelings. Darcy reveals a surprising susceptibility to Elizabeth, and once more what is overheard is important to the gradual development of relationships. Mary continues boring and pompous; Sir William boring and obsequious. His questions of Darcy are indicative of his small snobbery. Elizabeth shows her spirit and obstinacy in refusing to dance with Darcy – her 'pride and prejudice' are both involved. Her appraisal of Miss Bingley is confirmed by that lady's reception of Darcy's praise of a 'pair of fine eyes' (p.19), and also her insensitivity in talking at Darcy, for 'as his composure convinced her that all was safe, her wit flowed long'. (p.19).

fixing him i.e. tying him down.
Vingt-un . . . Commerce Both are card games.
felicity Happiness.
it is better to know as little as possible of the defects of the person with whom you are to pass your life This is very ironic in view of the fact that Charlotte marries Mr Collins, whose defects are trying and various.
concerto Unusual usage, here meaning of course the solo playing of music. Normally it would involve an orchestra or at least a group of musicians.
science i.e. dancing.
complaisance Willing agreement.
when am I to wish you joy? i.e. when am I to congratulate you on your engagement?

Chapter 7

An account of Mr Bennet's property being entailed on a distant relation is followed by the news that a militia regiment is stationed at the neighbouring town of Meryton. The two younger girls, Kitty and Lydia, visit Mrs Bennet's sister, Mrs Philips, regularly, their aim being to meet the officers. When they return from a visit, their gossipy news is overshadowed by an invitation to Jane from Bingley's sisters to stay with them at Netherfield while the gentlemen are dining with the officers. Jane goes on horseback, gets wet and catches a cold and, to Mrs Bennet's delight, has to remain at Netherfield. Her letter immediately moves Elizabeth to go to see her. She arrives at Netherfield muddy and dishevelled; Jane is anxious for her to remain, and, with some reserve, Miss Bingley invites Elizabeth to stay.

Commentary

Both the entail and the presence of the militia have important repercussions later in the plot. The incompatibility of Mr and Mrs Bennet is further indicated by their different evaluations of the 'effusions' of their silly daughters Catherine and Lydia. A fine dramatic stroke is provided by Miss Bingley's letter (note how often Jane Austen uses the letter in this novel) and by Jane's letter which, so to speak, plays into Mrs Bennet's hands by compelling Jane to remain at Netherfield and thus within easy access for Bingley. Elizabeth's rejection of convention, her natural concern and spirit, demands that she go to Netherfield; there is some delicious irony at the expense of Mr Hurst who is 'thinking only of his breakfast' (p.24). The thorough selfishness and snobbery of Miss Bingley is shown at the end of the chapter when she offers Elizabeth the use of the carriage. She has little real concern for Jane.

entailed . . . distant relation i.e. Mr Bennet's estate did not become his own property, and only a *male* relation could succeed to it.
militia regiment An auxiliary force of soldiers enlisted by the counties. They underwent periodical training and could be called out in an emergency. (Note that this novel is set during the period of the French Revolutionary Wars (1793–1815), when this country was threatened with invasion.)
regimentals of an ensign The uniform and insignia of an officer of the lowest rank.
sensible of it i.e. aware of it.
Clarke's library There were no public libraries at the time, but private libraries to which users subscribed in order to borrow books.
tête-à-tête Private conversation, generally between two people.
prognostics Forecasts.
in pursuit . . . under your orders Note that Mr Bennet's irony employs military terminology deliberately to describe Mrs Bennet's activities in the light of constant mention of the 'officers'.
the activity of your benevolence Note Mary's pompous and pedantically reasoned definition of Elizabeth's natural sympathy.
repaired Went to.
apothecary i.e. one who is allowed to prescribe drugs.
draughts Doses of medicine.

Chapter 8

Jane is nursed by Elizabeth, the latter being criticized by Bingley's sisters when she is out of the room. Neither Bingley nor Darcy responds to this. After visiting Jane briefly, the sisters play cards and Elizabeth joins them for a while with the gentlemen. There is talk of Darcy's sister and again some cattiness about Elizabeth when she is gone.

Commentary

Elizabeth is encouraged by the evident concern of Bingley on Jane's account, and the omnipresent irony conveys Elizabeth's 'enjoyment' at once more being in a position to dislike the obvious insincerity of Bingley's sisters. Once they begin to criticize Elizabeth we are aware of Bingley's sincerity and of Darcy's admiration for Elizabeth. The cards-books debate is an index to the morality of the speakers. The praise of Georgiana Darcy is calculated to undermine Elizabeth, but instead brings her into an animated discussion with Darcy on the nature of the truly accomplished woman. Miss Bingley's further attempt to undermine Elizabeth only draws from Darcy an enigmatic reply which rebounds on Miss Bingley herself. Dialogue throughout is easily natural and an accurate pointer to the character of each of the speakers.

complacency Satisfaction.
ragout Rich stew of meat or poultry and vegetables.
keep my countenance i.e. restrain myself, or maintain my own composure.
Cheapside An area of London known for its various trades. Bingley's sisters are being, as usual, snobbish.
loo A card game with stakes or forfeits – Elizabeth avoids it because they are 'playing high'.
skreens i.e. fire-screens, decorative screens.
net Make (from cotton, fabric etc).
comprehend a great deal Include many qualities.
Whatever bears affinity ... What is close to, identified with.
an express i.e. a quick message or request.

Chapter 9

Next morning Jane is somewhat better, and Mrs Bennet and her other daughters come to visit her. Mrs Bennet insists that Jane is too unwell to be moved and, in general conversation, misunderstands Darcy and displays her general vulgarity and illbreeding. Lydia shows her brashness in asking Bingley persistently to give a ball.

Commentary

Mrs Bennet is as talkative and determined as ever to promote the match between Jane and Bingley, and Elizabeth deduces from Bingley's concern that he is most sincerely attached to Jane. Mrs Bennet reveals her insensitivity, and Bingley reveals his own insecurity. Mrs Bennet causes laughter both by her vulgarity and her inability to understand, but there is a certain irony in her dwelling on Charlotte Lucas's plainness in view of that young lady's later marriage to Mr Collins. Elizabeth is sensitive to her mother's volubility, but has an intelligent interchange of remarks with Darcy. Miss Bingley is able to exhibit her cold snobbery to Mrs Bennet, and Lydia to show promise of her own irresponsibility to come. Like her mother, she is insensitive and vulgar and has 'a sort of natural self-consequence' (p.33) which is going to get her attention and trouble. Darcy further reveals his attachment to Elizabeth by refusing to criticize her.

chief Best part.
amendment Improvement.
'Whatever I do is done in a hurry . . .' This is prophetic, perhaps unconsciously at this stage, of the sudden decision to quit Netherfield later.
suffered Allowed.
quite as much of *that* going on Note Mrs Bennet's vulgarity as revealed in this remark, the *'that'* embodying unconsciously what she delights in – gossip.
she was wanted about i.e. she was needed for – implying that Charlotte has to do menial tasks, unlike her own daughters.
partiality i.e. prejudice in favour of.
to consider poetry as the *food* of love i.e. I have been used to think that poetry is the food for love – Darcy is perhaps echoing Orsino's words at the opening of Shakespeare's *Twelfth Night*: 'If music be the food of love, play on'.
one good sonnet Elizabeth is being very sarcastic, sonnets – particularly popular in the Elizabethan period – being largely artificial rather than sincere expressions of love.

Chapter 10

Miss Bingley constantly pesters Darcy while he is writing to his sister Georgiana. All engage in conversation, with Elizabeth joining in the friendly disagreement between Bingley and Darcy which becomes a little heated. While Miss Bingley plays and Mrs

Hurst sings, Darcy talks to Elizabeth and 'had never been so bewitched by any woman as he was by her' (p.38). The next day Miss Bingley's jealousy is apparent, but Elizabeth's only concern is to return home with Jane.

Commentary

Miss Bingley is intent on flattering Darcy, and there is a fine contrast between her voluble commentary and Darcy's terse replies. He is not terse with Bingley, however, but provocative and insightful, pointing out how Bingley's decisions depend on the whims of chance. What he is really revealing – and this is important – is Bingley's susceptibility to influence and also his impulsive nature. The debate on the influence of one friend on another is at the centre of the developing plot of the novel, for Darcy is to influence Bingley away from Netherfield and Jane. Elizabeth, as always, displays her good sense and rational judgement. She notes Darcy's eyes are frequently watching her, but 'She liked him too little to care for his approbation' (p.38). Nevertheless she is 'amazed at his gallantry' (p.38). Miss Bingley, jealous, tries to undermine Elizabeth's influence on Darcy by constant reference to the vulgarity of her relations.

piquet Card game for two people playing with a reduced pack.
mend it for you i.e. your quill pen, the feather of which would have to be sharpened or 'mended'.
panegyric Public praise, a eulogy written in praise of (ironic here).
precipitance . . . celerity Haste, speed.
without conviction Not being convinced.
appertain Be attached.
indulgence Pleasure.
reel Any of a number of lively Scottish dances.
compass it Bring it about.
lines i.e. positions – implying here that they are of a lower status.
to have it taken i.e. a portrait or sketch (of Elizabeth).
uncommon advantage i.e. you are just right as you are – to admit a fourth – herself – would spoil the balance.

Revision questions on Chapters 1–10

1 Write a character study of Mr Bennet as he appears in some of these chapters.

2 Compare and contrast Bingley and Darcy.

3 By close attention to what she says, give an account of Mrs Bennet's role in the novel so far.

4 In what ways is Elizabeth the 'moral centre' of the book in these early chapters?

5 Write an essay on Jane Austen's use of dialogue in any single chapter.

6 Discuss either (a) jealousy or (b) snobbery in the novel so far.

7 Write on any other aspect of *Pride and Prejudice* which has interested you so far.

Chapter 11

Jane is so much improved after dinner that she joins the others; Bingley is all attentiveness to her, while Miss Bingley continues her shameless pursuit of Darcy. She tries to distract him from his book, and then to persuade her brother not to give a ball at Netherfield. Miss Bingley persuades Elizabeth to walk up and down the room with her, but Elizabeth, though she joins her, manages to have an argument with Darcy in which she accuses him of 'implacable resentment' and 'a propensity to hate everybody' (p. 43) while he accuses her of wilful misunderstanding. Darcy fears that he is paying too much attention to Elizabeth.

Commentary

As long as the ladies are alone Miss Bingley and her sister are kind to Jane. With the appearance of the gentlemen, Miss Bingley is absorbed in Darcy, Bingley in impetuous 'joy and attention' (p. 41), and Mr Hurst, after the refusal of cards, in sleep. Miss Bingley reveals herself a hypocrite over reading; Darcy reveals his strength of will in his concentration. She walks to show off her figure, the irony being that Darcy of course becomes engrossed by Elizabeth's. Darcy penetrates Miss Bingley's motives for such display – how well he knows her! – while the argument between Darcy and Elizabeth reveals both their pride and their prejudice. Elizabeth is continuing to judge on 'first impressions' but Darcy, while noting her prejudice, is obviously fascinated by her independence of spirit and vivacity.

diffuseness i.e. uttering many expressions.
petition Request.
cards i.e. of invitation.
puffed about i.e. variable, uncertain.

Chapter 12

Although Mrs Bennet is against the girls returning to Longbourn, Elizabeth is determined. They leave on the Sunday; Bingley is grieved, Darcy relieved, and the sisters delighted. They are received rather coldly by their mother, who was hoping that they would have remained away longer, but Mr Bennet is pleased to see them and Catherine (Kitty) and Lydia are anxious to give them the latest news of the officers.

Commentary

Elizabeth displays her determination, Jane shows that she is susceptible to the false concern of Bingley's sisters, and Darcy reveals his own susceptibility towards Elizabeth and his fear of his own conduct if she should stay longer. He displays great restraint in hardly speaking to her. Miss Bingley acts in character throughout, as does Mrs Bennet, since her plans have been frustrated. We note the genuine pleasure of Mr Bennet – after all, these two girls represent what sense there is in his house.

propitious Promising.
laconic Seemingly casual, not vital.
felt Missed.
thorough bass The theory of harmony, with particular reference to the bass portion of the work.
a private had been flogged Note how Kitty and Lydia lump this in with the gossip – it shows their insensitivity.

Chapter 13

Mr Bennet tells the family that his cousin, the heir to the estate, has written a letter announcing that he will be visiting them and staying for a while. The letter is given in full, and when Mr

Collins appears he lives up to its tone; he is a boring, pompous young man who is obsequiously proud of the patronage of Lady Catherine de Bourgh, the widow of a knight who has presented him with the living of Hunsford in Kent.

Commentary

There is much humour, conveyed through Mr Bennet's quiet irony at the beginning of this chapter, as well as Mrs Bennet's mistaking the visitor who is coming for Mr Bingley. Note the time Mr Bennet takes to reply to Mr Collins's letter – an indication of his wish to lead a quiet life. Mrs Bennet's response before she hears the letter is typically irrational. The letter itself – and I have already drawn attention to the use Jane Austen makes of letters – is a masterpiece of pompous condescension, pedantically worded, complacent, conceited, snobbish: the words are the man. Both Elizabeth and her father see through it. Mr Collins's praise of everything he sees shows his insincere flattery and, as Mrs Bennet suspects, his proprietary interest. Her chief hope is fixed, as always, on the idea that he has come to marry one of the girls.

iniquitous Wicked, unjust.
patronage . . . has preferred i.e. many of the livings presented to clergymen were in the gift of a nobleman or a person of wealth. Note that where Mr Collins is fortunate, Wickham claims to have been badly treated in a similar situation, since he at one time expected a living from the Darcy family.
highly commendable Note the self-satisfaction in the tone.
the offered olive branch Mr Collins naturally descends into cliché.
Saturday se'nnight following i.e. Saturday week.
sensible Elizabeth is being ironic, punning on sensible. Here she means that Mr Collins is (a) being insensitive and (b) isn't very intelligent or aware.
asperity Sharpness.

Chapter 14

After dinner Mr Bennet engages Mr Collins in conversation and learns much of Lady Catherine de Bourgh and of her daughter. Later Mr Collins bores the girls by reading Fordyce's *Sermons* to them, is interrupted by Lydia and afterwards plays backgammon with Mr Bennet.

Commentary

All Mr Collins's pomposity, self-importance and excessive obsequiousness to Lady Catherine are brought out in this delightful
chapter, with Mr Bennet cleverly drawing out Mr Collins to even
greater absurdities, praising his 'talent of flattering with delicacy'
(p. 50). He is aware of Elizabeth's silent participation in his
enjoyment that 'His cousin was as absurd as he hoped' (pp.
50–51). Lydia again shows her forwardness and insensitivity,
though the reader might agree that interrupting Mr Collins is
justifiable.

pool of quadrille A card game for four players.
little phaeton Light open carriage having four wheels.
May I ask . . . Note the deliberate, weighted and witty irony of Mr
  Bennet here.
novels i.e. considered to be light reading. Jane Austen elevated the
  status of the novel by her own moral and literary concerns in her
  writing.
Fordyce's Sermons *Sermons to Young Women*, by James Fordyce.

Chapter 15

Mr Collins obviously has marriage to one of the girls in view, and
learns from Mrs Bennet that Jane is 'likely to be very soon
engaged' (p. 53). He changes quickly to Elizabeth, and goes for a
walk with his cousins. They meet an officer, Mr Denny, who
introduces them to a newly-joined brother officer, Mr Wickham,
a very attractive man. While they are talking to them Bingley
and Darcy ride up to the group; Darcy and Wickham are mutu-
ally embarrassed by the meeting. Afterwards Mr Collins and the
girls go to Mr Philips's house, Mr Collins being very pleased with
his reception by the girls' aunt, who invites them to dine there
the next day.

Commentary

Further emphasis on Mr Collins's conceit and of his shallow
nature – 'Mr Collins had only to change from Jane to Elizabeth –
and it was soon done – done while Mrs Bennet was stirring the
fire' (p.53). The impact of Wickham, the narrative tension
heightened by his meeting with Darcy and by the knowledge

that he too is to be invited by Mrs Philips the next evening, establishes the plot links which are to reach right forward into the action of the novel.

kept the necessary terms i.e. attended.
pleasing address Manner and mode of conducting himself.

Chapter 16

Mr Collins is able to condescend and talk to Mrs Philips, and Wickham joins Elizabeth. In the course of their conversation he reveals that Darcy has treated him very badly and (supposedly) broken the elder Mr Darcy's promises to him. Elizabeth responds sympathetically to his disclosures, and expresses her indignation on his account. Later, after observing Mr Collins, Wickham further reveals that Lady Catherine de Bourgh is Darcy's aunt, and that Darcy and her daughter are expected to marry. Wickham has impressed everybody, particularly Elizabeth.

Commentary

Mr Collins is eclipsed (though not in his own mind of course) by Wickham. The latter talks freely – we might think too freely on so short an acquaintance – to Elizabeth. She reveals her own susceptibility (it is the first fault we note in her) to persuasive talk and the natural attractions of Wickham. The whole conversation between them, with Wickham's revelations, should be studied carefully, since it shows the subtlety with which Jane Austen presents character, here the willing 'prejudice' of Elizabeth and the danger of hearing one side of an argument only. Later, of course, Elizabeth is to reflect on this. The power of rumour and false deduction is shown in Wickham's report that Darcy is to marry Lady Catherine's daughter, but note the balancing truth, as we are later to find out, in his description of Lady Catherine.

imitations of china Plain china which had been decorated by amateurs.
muffin Round backed yeast roll, usually toasted.
whist A very popular card game for four people.
country i.e. area, county.
the delicacy of it i.e. the sensitive nature of what they were discussing.
the living fell i.e. became available.

'It *is* wonderful . . . i.e. it is very surprising.
cried up Spoken of approvingly.
want abilities Lack social talents.
conversible i.e. able to carry on a conversation.
allowing something for fortune and figure i.e. provided that they are
  rich and attractive in presence.
allowed Admitted.
the fish she had lost i.e. the counters (in the shapes of fish) which she
  had lost in her game.
crouded i.e. was giving his cousins little room in the carriage.

Chapter 17

Jane is disconcerted by Elizabeth's account of what Wickham has
said, but this soon gives way to the excitement of having Bingley
and his sisters call with a personal invitation to the ball at
Netherfield on the following Tuesday. All look forward to this,
including Mr Collins, who has no clerical scruples about going,
and even asks Elizabeth for the first two dances. The weather is
bad. Elizabeth receives a hint from her mother that Mr Collins
wants to marry her (Elizabeth).

Commentary

Jane's simple generosity of feeling is shown in her reception of
Wickham's revelations – she finds it difficult to believe evil of
anybody. Elizabeth, as we have seen, shows her prejudice by
presupposing that Wickham is telling the truth. We note the
various reactions to the ball – Elizabeth looking forward to being
with Wickham, Mrs Bennet assuming that the ball is being given
as a compliment to Jane, the eager anticipation of multiple
conquests by Kitty and Lydia, and the pompous pronounce-
ments of Mary – 'Society has claims on us all' (p. 65). Elizabeth
has the tact to ignore her mother's hint, though she sees clearly
that Mr Collins has selected her 'as worthy of being the mistress
of Hunsford Parsonage' (p. 66). The incessant rain is almost a
forecasting symbol of what is to come in the sense that Jane's life,
and for a while Elizabeth's, are to be overcast.

misrepresented each to the either i.e. those concerned with self-gain
  had spread lies.
taken in i.e. accidently in an awkward position.
per force Unavoidably.

shoe-roses Ornaments for the shoes, probably made from ribbon.
by proxy i.e. had to be purchased for them (since they couldn't go in to
  Meryton because of the rain).

Chapter 18

Elizabeth is surprised to find that Wickham is not at the Netherfield ball; initially irritated, she talks with Charlotte, then
endures Mr Collins, learns more of Wickham from another
officer, and then – despite herself – dances with Darcy. She
reveals her sympathy for Wickham and disconcerts Darcy by so
doing. Meanwhile Sir William Lucas hints at the coming
engagement of Jane and Bingley; this strikes Darcy 'forcibly' (p.
70). Miss Bingley then tells Elizabeth about Wickham. Elizabeth
learns from Jane that Bingley does not doubt Darcy's honour in
the Wickham affair and they talk happily of Jane's prospects.
Elizabeth then has to endure the ill-breeding of Mr Collins who
insists on introducing himself to Mr Darcy. To cap this, Mrs
Bennet is rude about Darcy within his hearing. Mary makes
herself a nuisance by boring the company with her singing, Mr
Collins bores them with his reasons as to why he does not sing.
Simply, the Bennet family overstay their welcome. They are the
last to leave.

Commentary

An important chapter in the plot, with one event following
another. Only Elizabeth and Jane acquit themselves well (Mr
Bennet is merely amused by what goes on) for the rest of the
family blight themselves in the eyes of Darcy and Bingley's
sisters, and this undoubtedly leads Darcy to persuade Bingley to
leave Netherfield later. Wickham's absence is suspicious in itself,
but naturally Elizabeth interprets it in the way she wishes to. 'But
Elizabeth was not formed for ill-humour' (p. 67) shows us the
unmalicious nature of the girl. Her dancing with Darcy brings
back all her spirit and, certainly, shows us Darcy as rather shy of
her. She is playful (despite her inner prejudice) and provocative
when she mentions Wickham. The interruption of Sir William
undoubtedly sets Darcy's mind working, and his coldness is
excusable when one considers Elizabeth's emphasis on his –
Darcy's – prejudice and resentment. For once Miss Bingley is

right, or is later proved to be right, about Wickham. Here Elizabeth is rather headstrong – she believes of Wickham what she wants to believe.

The central part of this chapter, however, deals with the let-down provided by Mr Collins, then by Mrs Bennet, who talks of the certainty of the engagement of Jane and Bingley. Most of these words are heard by Darcy, himself somewhat offended already by Elizabeth and also rather frightened of his feelings for her. Mary contributes her own mite to the family obloquy, while Mr Collins attaches himself to Elizabeth, the latter being somewhat protected by Charlotte – it is a subtle preparation on Jane Austen's part for Mr Collins's sudden move later from the former to the latter. There is also the irony and insensitivity of Mrs Bennet in her complacency at the end of the chapter.

blind partiality Unthinking preference.
refreshment i.e. exultation.
without knowing what she did . . . Elizabeth's dancing with Darcy is perhaps suggestive of her subconscious but unacknowledged liking for him.
by rule According to set convention.
éclat Effect, success.
hauteur Haughtiness.
descent Is Miss Bingley punning? She obviously means his lower birth, and perhaps also his 'descent' in the world.
probity Integrity.
consequence Status.
wonder Amazement.
self-gratulation i.e. self-satisfaction.
intelligible i.e. which could be understood – and heard.
proof of complaisance Evidence of self-conceit.
tythes Contributions in tenths made voluntarily or as a tax for the support of the clergy.
exhibition i.e. Mr Collins's – and Mrs Bennet's – vulgar display of themselves.
engaged for i.e. pledged himself.

Chapter 19

Having got Mrs Bennet's willing support, Mr Collins proceeds to propose to Elizabeth. His main motivation is the wish of Lady Catherine that he should marry. Elizabeth rejects him forth-rightly, but Mr Collins feels that she is merely being coy.

Summoning all her spirited powers Elizabeth tries to make him understand that she is serious; she fails, and thinks that if he persists she will have to enlist the help of her father.

Commentary

Mrs Bennet is only too eager to leave Mr Collins with her daughter; Elizabeth is reduced to pleading with her mother. Mr Collins's proposal 'in form' is masterly in its pomposity, self-conceit, condescension, crawling subjection to Lady Catherine. He even knows that Elizabeth has an inheritance on her mother's death! His arrogance will not let him entertain a refusal, although he pauses when Elizabeth, using a cunning blackmail, tells him that if Lady Catherine knew her 'she would find me in every respect ill-qualified for the situation' (p. 81). Mr Collins blindly attributes Elizabeth's attitude to 'the usual practice of elegant females' (p. 82). There is no puncturing this caricature of a man; his image of himself is never blemished.

in form i.e. formally.
interest i.e. support.
injunction Command.
diversion Elizabeth is here referring to her own inward amusement at the ridiculousness of the situation.
dissemble i.e. pretend not to know.
pools at quadrille See note p. 29
You will find her manners beyond anything I can describe Mr Collins is completely unaware of the irony in his description – Lady Catherine's manners are as condescending, arrogant and snobbish as his own.
the violence of my affection We note that Mr Collins's violent affection soon changes.
To fortune i.e. Elizabeth's dowry.
the 4 per cents The investment in government stock which brought in 4% interest annually.
'I am not now to learn' i.e. 'I already know'.
portion Fortune, inheritance.

Chapter 20

Mrs Bennet is annoyed (and alarmed) to learn that Elizabeth has rejected Mr Collins's proposal; she insists that Mr Bennet shall use his authority to bring about the match. He does, but not in the way that Mrs Bennet expects; he finds Elizabeth determined, and tells her that she is in a very awkward position, since her mother is going to refuse to see her again if she does not marry Mr Collins, while he, her father, will never see her again if she does. Mrs Bennet takes out her exasperation on Elizabeth in the presence of Lydia and Charlotte Lucas, and Mr Collins tells Mrs Bennet that he no longer has any wish to marry Elizabeth.

Commentary

The irony plays over Mr Collins's 'successful love' (p. 83), for such it is in his own mind, and Mrs Bennet makes the situation worse by describing Elizabeth as 'a very headstrong, foolish girl' (p. 84), thus putting doubts into Mr Collins's mind about her suitability. Notice how the drama of Mr Bennet's interview with Elizabeth is turned into the delightful humour occasioned by his classic wit on the choices lying before Elizabeth. Mrs Bennet has recourse to her 'nerves', but Mr Collins, who has meditated in silence, adds injured pride to his pompous oratory.

vestibule Small entrance hall.
know her own interest i.e. what is good for her.
in her interest i.e. on her side.
than if we were at York i.e. if we were miles away.
effusion Outpouring.
preferment Promotion, holding a good position.
dismission i.e. rejection.

Revision questions on Chapters 11–20

1 Write a detailed account of Elizabeth's stay at Netherfield.

2 What do you find humorous in (a) Mr Collins's letter and (b) Mr Collins himself in these chapters?

3 Write an essay on Elizabeth's 'pride and prejudice' in these chapters.

4 Examine the part played by (a) Wickham and (b) Mrs Philips when they appear.

5 Give an account of the significant happenings at the Netherfield ball.

6 Describe Mr Collins's proposal to Elizabeth and its effects.

Chapter 21

Mr Collins stays in 'angry pride', the girls go to Meryton and meet Wickham, who explains why he avoided Darcy. Jane receives a letter from Caroline Bingley saying that the whole family have gone to London and will not be returning for some time. She also writes that Bingley, they hope, will become engaged to Georgiana Darcy, Darcy's sister. Jane is obviously upset by the news but continues to think well of Caroline Bingley. Elizabeth thinks that Caroline is after Darcy for herself, and that Bingley will return.

Commentary

This chapter prepares us for Mr Collins's soon-to-be-announced engagement to Charlotte Lucas and his obstinacy in staying his time out where he is not wanted. Wickham's glibness in fact convinces Elizabeth of his sincerity, while Caroline Bingley's letter shows Jane's sensitivity and loyalty and, of course, Caroline's hypocrisy. She is intent on stirring things up, with particular reference to the supposed match between her brother and Georgiana Darcy. Elizabeth, always rational (accept at this stage with regard to Wickham), tries to restore Jane's morale, with some success. Mrs Bennet, annoyed over Elizabeth's refusal of Mr Collins, is further upset by Bingley's sudden departure but, ever optimistic, anticipates his quick return.

hot-pressed paper Paper made glossy by being placed between hot plates.
the insensibility of distrust i.e. makes Elizabeth insensitive to Miss Bingley's over-emotional writing – she disbelieves her sincerity.
beaux i.e. young men who will pay court to her.

Chapter 22

Mr Collins quickly transfers his attentions to Charlotte Lucas, who is only too happy to become his wife. Sir William and Lady Lucas are delighted to have a daughter advantageously situated. On hearing the news from Charlotte, Elizabeth is astounded, though Mr Collins, without revealing his engagement, has also surprised the Bennet family by announcing that he will soon be returning. Charlotte reveals that she is not romantic and is, in fact, marrying for security.

Commentary

This chapter is full of fine irony, with Charlotte determined to encourage Mr Collins, even meeting him 'accidently in the lane'. One of the main motifs of the novel is being sounded – the need for families with daughters to see them married. Charlotte's views are ironically expressed as 'marriage had always been her object'. She behaves honourably in asking her fiancé to keep the engagement secret for the time being. Mr Collins is at his pedantic best in announcing his speedy return, the thought of which moves Mr Bennet to dry humour of his own since he cannot bear the thought of it. There is a kind of dramatic irony here too, since the reader knows what the Bennets do not know, that Mr Collins is engaged. Elizabeth's reactions are understandable, but she tones them down in order not to hurt her friend. Mr Collins is fully exposed – his sole reason for the visit to Longbourn was to get himself married suitably in order to further his position with his patroness.

the chief of the day Most of the day.
secure i.e. protect (Elizabeth) because she wants Mr Collins for herself.
coming out i.e. being presented in society.
grateful Pleasing.

Chapter 23

Mrs Bennet is quite distraught at the news of the engagement though Elizabeth tries to get her to see it in its proper perspective. Mr Bennet meanwhile is relieved to learn he will not have Mr Collins inflicted on him as a son-in-law. Elizabeth turns increasingly to Jane, who is of course worried about the continued absence of Bingley. Mr Collins is coolly received by the Bennets on his return, but his insensitivity is not affected by their attitude.

Commentary

A finely dramatic opening to the chapter, with Sir William's announcement and Mrs Bennet's unbelieving acceptance of it. Elizabeth's attempts to right matters are doomed to failure, but as always it is her common sense and rationality which stand out. Mrs Bennet typically lays the blame at Elizabeth's door, and is self-dramatic and self-pitying at the thought of Charlotte being the future mistress of Longbourn. There is some delightfully ironic dialogue between Mr and Mrs Bennet, but we also notice that Jane is already going into a decline at the prospect of Bingley's non-return.

complaisance of a courtier Note the irony – Sir William is not a
  courtier but is mindful of the dignity of his position, which carries him
  through.
retort on Triumph over.
rectitude Uprightness, integrity.

Chapter 24

Miss Bingley's letter makes it clear that the family will be remaining in London for the winter, and Jane gives way to her feelings to Elizabeth, though still refuses to blame Bingley. They see Wickham much, and he continues to spread the account of Darcy's ill-treatment of him, so much so that Darcy is generally condemned – of course, in his absence.

Commentary

Miss Bingley's letter upsets Jane but such is her reserve that she takes two days to communicate her feelings to Elizabeth. The latter is indignant, and Jane's reactions are not helped by the insensitivity of her mother. Jane shows how genuinely good she is by still refusing to blame Bingley; Elizabeth ponders on 'the inconsistency of all human characters', Jane even defends Charlotte's marriage to Mr Collins on the grounds of his 'respectability', but Elizabeth doesn't hesitate to speak her mind about that pompous man. Mr Bennet continues his sly irony, somewhat insensitive here we feel, to Elizabeth at the expense of Jane – 'your sister is crossed in love, I find. I congratulate her'. The author's own irony is employed to expose Wickham's indiscretion and the response it gets from those he tells.

caprice Whim, sudden act.
unaccountable i.e. cannot be explained.
circumspect Cautious.
repine Fret.
material service Help.

Chapter 25

Mr Collins leaves Longbourn, and Mr and Mrs Gardiner the brother and sister-in-law of Mrs Bennet, arrive, to be greeted with Mrs Bennet's grievances. Elizabeth and Mrs Gardiner discuss Jane's situation, with Mrs Gardiner proposing to invite Jane to London for a while. She also learns from Wickham news of her former acquaintances in Derbyshire, since she had spent some time there before her marriage.

Commentary

We learn a little of Mr Gardiner – 'a sensible, gentlemanlike man' and more of his 'amiable, intelligent, elegant' wife. She shows her tact by turning away from Mrs Bennet's complaints, and obviously enjoys Elizabeth's conversation. She also shows her generosity of spirit in offering to take Jane to town in order to help her get over Bingley, while Elizabeth shows her shrewdness in saying that Miss Bingley will drop all contact with Jane even if she is within reach. Mrs Gardiner enjoys her exchange with Wickham but at the same time is 'uneasy' about his relationship with Elizabeth.

ablution i.e. washing, getting rid of the atmosphere (the implication is that Darcy's a snob – ironic in view of what happens when he does meet the Gardiners).
procuring Learning.

Chapter 26

Mrs Gardiner duly warns Elizabeth about Wickham, and suggests that she discourages him from visiting them so often. Elizabeth has character enough not to resent the advice. Charlotte leaves, her wedding to Mr Collins takes place, and she writes to Elizabeth. Meanwhile Jane, in London, writes to Elizabeth and, having visited Caroline Bingley and had that visit coldly returned, sees at last that Elizabeth has been right about her 'friend's' character. Elizabeth writes to Mrs Gardiner that Wickham's attentions to her have declined, and that he has transferred his attentions to an heiress, Miss King.

Commentary

The reaction of Elizabeth to Mrs Gardiner's caution is typically sensible, honest, her real character shown by her lack of resentment. Her sensitivity is further displayed as she shows her consciousness of her mother's lack of good manners before Charlotte leaves to be married. There is some pathos here as Charlotte, knowing that she is going to a life of secure boredom, wishes ardently to keep up her contact with Elizabeth. Here Jane Austen focuses on the passage of time and the changes that it brings – the first letters from Charlotte and the crucial letter from Jane which show how much she is suffering. Letters are important narrative or crisis points in *Pride and Prejudice*. Wickham's essential opportunism is exposed.

in spirits i.e. happy, content.
duplicity Deceit.
partiality Preference.

Chapter 27

In March Elizabeth, Sir William Lucas and his daughter Maria go off to visit the Collinses. On the way they stay with the Gardiners in London. They shop, go to the theatre, but the main narrative concerns Mrs Gardiner's teasing Elizabeth about her loss of Wickham, the depression suffered by Jane on account of the Bingleys, and a projected visit to the Lake district in the summer, with Elizabeth invited to join her aunt and uncle.

Commentary

This is swift narrative movement. Again two or three months are quickly glossed over. Elizabeth genuinely wants to see Charlotte – and acknowledges that she wants to get away from her mother and sisters. She endures the boring Sir William, is concerned for Jane, and there is some delightful humour between her aunt and herself at the 'fickle' nature of Wickham. Elizabeth responds excitedly, a mark of her spirited naturalness at the thought of something new, a visit to the Lakes.

solicitude Concern.
chaise i.e. the horse-drawn carriage.

the Lakes i.e. the Lake District, where the Romantic poets –
  Wordsworth, Coleridge, Southey – were settled about this time.
  Elizabeth is being satirical (though she wants to go) about the ecstatic
  praise given to the area by some travellers.
spleen Ill-humour.
transport Delight.
effusions Extravagant praises.

Chapter 28

The arrival at Hunsford is described with Charlotte delighted to
see her family and friend and Mr Collins as pompous as ever –
much to Elizabeth's amusement. On the following day Elizabeth
sees Lady Catherine's paid companion and Miss de Bourgh
arrive at the gate. She is rather amused at the 'condescension' of
this and also notes that Miss de Bourgh is 'sickly and cross'.

Commentary

There is a finely ironic account of Mr Collins's formality, which
is obviously aimed at showing Elizabeth what she has missed by
not marrying him. She notes too Charlotte's sensitivity to her
husband's blunders. There is genuine humour in the bowing
and scraping attitude of Mr Collins towards anything associated
with his patroness, and even more in Elizabeth's notice of Miss
de Bourgh who, she feels, will suit Darcy well. There is a neat
little focus too on the constant bowing of Sir William, 'in earnest
contemplation of the greatness before him'.

command of countenance i.e. control of her features (and
  expressions).
affability and condescension i.e. friendliness and acceptance, (but
  with an ironic stab at her awareness of rank).
my sister Maria i.e. sister-in-law.
her address in guiding i.e. the application of her skill.

Chapter 29

The talk before, and then the description of, the visit to Rosings.
Lady Catherine is described, as is her sickly daughter, and after
the dinner Lady Catherine proceeds to dominate the conversation. Elizabeth, indeed, has to endure a form of condescending
interrogation from this formidable woman.

Commentary

The fussing of Mr Collins and the nervousness of Sir William and Maria are complemented by the straightforward naturalness and good sense of Elizabeth. She finds Wickham's description of Lady Catherine to be true; she is an authoritative and self important – and ill-bred – woman. The praise of the dinner is markedly satirical, Mr Collins and Sir William sucking up to rank unashamedly. Lady Catherine's questions of Elizabeth are impertinent, but Elizabeth matches her inquisitiveness at every turn, even to the point of independent and disconcerting answers to this self-assertive dictator. In the background we note the pathos of poor sickly Miss de Bourgh.

trepidation Fear, apprehension.
composedly i.e. without feeling worried.
deportment i.e. the way she carried or held herself.
never wanted the means i.e. never lacked the equipment.
every fish he won See note in Chapter 16 on p. 31 of this book.

Chapter 30

Sir William returns home at the end of the week. Mr Collins employs himself about his usual occupations of walking to Rosings, and they dine there about twice a week. Lady Catherine interferes and manages every detail of the Collins's life that she can. We soon learn that Darcy and another cousin, Colonel Fitzwilliam, are coming to visit their aunt Lady Catherine at Easter. On their arrival they come over to the parsonage, and Elizabeth asks Darcy if he has seen her sister in London. She feels that he is a little confused by the question.

Commentary

Further extensive underlining of the sycophancy of Mr Collins and the magisterial authority of Lady Catherine. There is delightful irony at the fact that 'this great lady was not in the commission of the peace for this county'. Hints of future plot developments are given in Elizabeth's walking alone in the park, and of the arrival of Darcy and Colonel Fitzwilliam. Note how Jane Austen succeeds in raising narrative tension through the briefest of exchanges – that between Elizabeth and Darcy, for instance – so that we are left in expectation that something will happen.

gig Small carriage.
backwards At the rear of the house.
family livings i.e. Mr Collins might get an even better church gift – or even another one – which his patroness could provide.
intelligence News.

Revision questions on Chapters 21–30

1 In what ways do you feel sorry for Charlotte Collins over the course of these chapters?

2 Write an essay showing that Elizabeth is both independent and sensitive. Refer to the text closely in your answer.

3 Compare and contrast Mrs Gardiner with Lady Catherine de Bourgh.

4 Write an essay on Jane Austen's use of irony in these chapters.

5 Write an appreciation of any one scene which you consider important in these chapters.

Chapter 31

On Easter Day the Parsonage party are invited to Rosings, and Colonel Fitzwilliam soon becomes engrossed with Elizabeth. Lady Catherine interrupts their conversation constantly, Darcy being ashamed of his aunt's ill-breeding, and he engages Elizabeth in conversation. She teases him about his dancing only four times at the Netherfield ball, but has her piano playing in turn criticized by Lady Catherine.

Commentary

Lady Catherine displays her rudeness throughout while Colonel Fitzwilliam reveals genuine breeding and kindliness. Darcy softens towards Elizabeth; he reveals his pride in his sister, but shows no interest in Miss de Bourgh. Elizabeth is both spirited and witty in conversation with Darcy, and it is obvious that he is still attracted by her. Colonel Fitzwilliam reveals that Darcy is reserved and he himself allows that he hasn't the natural ease to recommend himself to strangers. Elizabeth receives Lady Catherine's comments 'with all the forbearance of civility', another instance of true breeding exposing the snobbery of rank.

Chapter 32

Darcy calls the next morning and finds Elizabeth alone. She questions him about Bingley's intentions with regard to Nether-field. They also discuss the Collins' marriage, but Darcy's man-ner surprises Elizabeth. Charlotte tells her friend that Darcy must be in love with her (Elizabeth). Darcy and Fitzwilliam pay frequent visits to the parsonage, and the kindly Charlotte even feels that perhaps Fitzwilliam may propose to Elizabeth.

Commentary

The fine narrative art sets up in the reader's mind the expecta-tion of Darcy's love for Elizabeth although she, with typical lack of conceit, laughs it off. She is concerned for Jane; Darcy on his visits is subdued, Charlotte kind.

Chapter 33

On her walks in the park Elizabeth often encounters Darcy, though little is said. Once she meets Colonel Fitzwilliam, and for a moment thinks that he may be in love with her. But this is put aside when Fitzwilliam reveals to her that Darcy has 'lately saved a friend' from a young lady against whom there were 'strong objections'. Elizabeth is greatly distressed by this.

Commentary

This chapter confirms Darcy's interest in Elizabeth and, ironically, shows her, after Fitzwilliam's account of Darcy's influence on Bingley, even more injured and set against him than ever because of his 'prejudice'. This is added to by another of Jane's letters which reflect her depression. Elizabeth puts down Darcy's rescue of Bingley to his snobbery. There is further irony in that Elizabeth unconsciously refers to the trouble Geor-giana has caused without realizing that this is to be laid later at

Wickham's door. Fitzwilliam unwittingly reveals in his turn that Darcy's rescue of Bingley must not 'get round to the lady's family'! Elizabeth is now convinced of Darcy's obdurate 'pride', and at the same time shows her own on Jane's account.

rencontre Meeting.
enured Used to.

Chapter 34

Elizabeth re-reads Jane's letters, but is surprised by a sudden visitor in the shape of Darcy himself. He tells her that he has struggled in vain against his love for her for some time. He asks her to marry him, but Elizabeth feeling his condescension and pride, and astonished 'beyond expression', knows that he expects an affirmative reply. She is direct in her refusal, and he accuses her of not even being civil; Elizabeth hits back by charging him with being the means of destroying her sister's happiness. Darcy admits that he separated Bingley from Jane, and Elizabeth follows this with an attack on him for injuring Wickham in the past. Incensed, Darcy dwells on her inferior connections, but Elizabeth tells him that she would not have accepted him in any case. Darcy leaves in anger, and Elizabeth is left in an emotional state.

Commentary

This is one of the highlights of the novel, the proposal of Darcy leading to confrontation and blunt words. Both Elizabeth and Darcy suffer from their pride and their prejudice, and the result is anger and bitterness. Elizabeth is secretly flattered but determined, Darcy proud and amazed at her response. We get beneath and into their characters in this exchange, and Elizabeth is injudicious to say the least in presenting Darcy's *supposed* treatment of Wickham as if it were fact. To use a modern phrase, she inexcusably 'goes over the top'. In turn Darcy reveals how he looks down on her family. This is a passionate scene, showing a keen insight into the responses and reactions of people who are moved by deep feelings.

consequence i.e. Elizabeth's own position and character.
derision Mocking laughter.

Chapter 35

Elizabeth meets Darcy in the park. He hands her a letter which explains his actions over Bingley and Wickham. With regard to Bingley, he says that although there was general talk of a marriage to Jane, he did not feel that Jane's emotions were completely involved. He also criticizes Mrs Bennet, the other sisters and their behaviour, and even Mr Bennet. He admits himself that he convinced Bingley of Jane's indifference, but also admits that he erred in not telling Bingley that Jane was in London. The rest of the letter is devoted to his account of Wickham's behaviour in the past, which was extravagant and dissolute, culminating in his attempt to elope with Georgiana, Darcy's sister. Darcy, however, prevented the elopement at the last minute. Darcy cites as evidence for what he says the word of Colonel Fitzwilliam, to whom Elizabeth can reply if she so wishes.

Commentary

We have already noted the use Jane Austen makes of letters, and this is the most masterly of them all. Darcy shows his integrity by writing in this way after the humiliation of his rejection. It is a letter in which he sinks his pride in order to convince Elizabeth of her prejudice, yet he is gracious enough to admit his own errors. It immediately raises him in our estimation. With superb narrative art, Jane Austen closes the chapter with the end of the letter, thus giving us breathing space before Elizabeth's reactions. Ironically, the original title of *Pride and Prejudice, First Impressions*, is reinvoked here; Darcy's first impressions of Jane's emotions were wrong, Elizabeth's first impressions of Wickham likewise.

turnpike road A road which has a toll-gate with a keeper who opened it on payment of a sum for coaches etc to pass through.
family living .. preferment i.e. within the gift of the Darcy family (which Wickham would get if he took holy orders).
for the presentation i.e. of the family living above.
establishment i.e. house or apartments of her own.

Chapter 36

Although Elizabeth disbelieves Darcy on the subject of Jane, she is forced to consider carefully the statements which relate to Wickham. Her second reading, Wickham's own indiscretion in talking so much to her, the knowledge that the criticisms of her family are justified, force her to see how blindly prejudiced she has been. She wanders about the lane, and when she returns learns that Darcy has called briefly to take his leave but that Colonel Fitzwilliam had sat an hour waiting for her.

Commentary

The pendulum of emotions on which Elizabeth swings is graphically conveyed in this chapter; the two readings reveal her first and second impressions. It is the stilling of her prejudice, the abeyance of her pride. Just as Darcy's letter ennobled him, so Elizabeth's responses ennoble her – she has integrity, honesty, thinks back over the past and her own faults and is scrupulously aware of her family's public impression. She also appreciates that Jane's unhappiness has been brought about by her own family.

contrariety of emotion Fluctuations in her feelings.
determining probabilities Trying to make out how things might have happened.

Chapter 37

After Darcy and Fitzwilliam have left, Lady Catherine tries dictatorially to get Elizabeth to prolong her stay and, finding that she won't, organizes her return journey, or rather, tries to. Elizabeth soon knows Darcy's letter practically by heart, and comes to the conclusion that her family have been seriously to blame. She is increasingly concerned for Jane.

Commentary

Lady Catherine's character and personality are seen to full effect, but Elizabeth is increasingly depressed by what she has learned from Darcy and by the unreasonableness of her own attitude towards him.

obeisance Bow.
Barouche box i.e. seat on the four-wheeled carriage.
affronted Angered.

Chapter 38

Mr Collins uses the occasion of Elizabeth's departure to utter a series of pompous addresses to her and to Maria, who retails to Elizabeth the number of things they will have to tell when they get home. Elizabeth ponders privately on what she will have to tell Jane.

Commentary

This short chapter is written with studied irony – the verbal flatulence of Mr Collins giving way to the naive and superficial reactions of Maria and the sorrow that Elizabeth feels at having to part from Charlotte, leaving her to the boredom of Mr Collins and the ever-present condescension of Lady Catherine. She also ponders, though she sees Jane looking well, on how much she should tell Jane, further evidence of her sensitivity on her sister's account.

commissioning i.e. telling her to give.

Chapter 39

Elizabeth and Jane are greeted by Kitty and Lydia with the news that the militia have left Meryton for a camp near Brighton. Mary King has gone to Liverpool, so that Wickham is still available, but Kitty and Lydia are trying to persuade their father to allow them to go on holiday to Brighton.

Commentary

This is an interim chapter to bring us up to date, and to arouse suspense in the reader before Elizabeth can give Jane her news. Lydia never stops talking and never listens. The discussion about the Brighton venture between her parents gives Elizabeth some disquiet, and the vulgarity of her sisters, together with the pretentious seriousness of Mary, is apparent to her.

affords Provides.
overset Overcome by.
bandbox i.e. for holding such articles as hats.
equivocal i.e. not firm, capable of being misunderstood.

Chapter 40

At last Elizabeth is able to tell Jane of Darcy's proposal and her rejection of it, and also what she has learned of Wickham's real character. Jane is shocked at the revelations about Wickham – after all, she will believe ill of nobody – but advises Elizabeth against exposing Wickham's character publicly. Elizabeth does not tell Jane about Bingley's sincere regard for her, though she sees that Jane is unhappy and obviously still thinks of him. Mrs Bennet questions Elizabeth about the Collins' way of life.

Commentary

This shows Jane's generosity of spirit, for she seeks to defend Wickham but also Darcy's integrity. She puts aside her own inner worries in order to give Elizabeth the sympathetic ear she needs. The moral responsibility of both girls is shown and Elizabeth, who has been the central focus of the novel, listens to Jane's good sense and right judgement. After this revelation, Mrs Bennet's vulgarity provides a strong contrast to the decency and responsibility of her daughters.

Revision questions on Chapters 31–40

1 In what ways are Elizabeth's feelings changed during her stay at Rosings?

2 Write an account of (a) Darcy's proposal scene with Elizabeth and (b) the main points of his letter to her after she has rejected him.

3 Write a short character sketch of (a) Colonel Fitzwilliam and (b) Lydia.

4 Illustrate the nature of Jane Austen's humour with reference to Mr Collins and Lady Catherine de Bourgh.

5 Justify the title *Pride and Prejudice* by reference to any three or four incidents in these chapters.

Chapter 41

The militia departs, but Lydia soon learns that she is to go to Brighton as the guest of the Forsters. Kitty is disconsolate, and

Elizabeth tries to persuade her father that it is irresponsible to let Lydia go. Mr Bennet, ever incapable of decision, feels that Lydia's flirtatiousness will be submerged by the number of girls in Brighton. Elizabeth now sees Wickham, reveals to him that she has met Darcy and Colonel Fitzwilliam at Rosings, and that she has found Darcy much improved. Wickham is put out by this, but accounts for it by saying that he suspects Darcy is furthering his courtship of Miss de Bourgh.

Commentary

This is an important chapter, since it gives Lydia the opportunity for temptation, reveals the active connivance of Mrs Bennet in promoting her daughter's schemes, and finds Mr Bennet singularly lacking in a right sense of moral perspective. Elizabeth herself displays a remarkably mature sense of that moral perspective when she pleads with her father not to let Lydia go. The irony is that the decision to let Lydia go will throw her into the company of Wickham; that gentleman is now almost seen in his true light and at the end of the chapter, Elizabeth lets him know that she *knows* what he is really like.

volatility i.e. swinging from one extreme to the other.

Chapter 42

Mrs Bennet and Kitty now find everything dull, and Elizabeth begins to look forward to her visit to the Lakes, while Lydia writes short and infrequent letters home. Meanwhile news comes from Mrs Gardiner that the date of their holiday has had to be changed because of her husband's business transactions, and that they are to tour Derbyshire instead. Though disappointed, Elizabeth naturally thinks of Darcy and his home, Pemberley, which is in that area. The time passes, and they set off, Mrs Gardiner, to Elizabeth's embarrassment, intent on visiting Pemberley.

Commentary

A keen insight into the character of Mr Bennet and his basic incompatibility, after their early married years, with Mrs Bennet. Elizabeth shows that she is not blind to her father's faults, but the main focus of this chapter is on the movement of time which quickly carries the plot forward, the change of tour for the holiday being a dramatic plot device to bring Elizabeth into interaction with Darcy.

repinings Complaints.
wanting of it i.e. (there was only) a fortnight to go.
Matlock On the river Derwent. It is celebrated for its mineral springs.
Chatsworth, Dovedale, or the Peak i.e. places they would visit in their
  tour of Derbyshire.

Chapter 43

Elizabeth has a good opportunity to admire the surroundings at Pemberley, and when they arrive there she is fascinated by the house itself. The housekeeper shows them round, obviously very proud of it and devoted to her master, Mr Darcy. Elizabeth sees a portrait of Wickham, and is informed by Mrs Reynolds that he has turned out 'very wild'. By contrast, Mrs Reynolds's own verbal portrait of Darcy shows that he is kind to his sister, the tenants, and the poor. They continue their inspection and on moving outside suddenly meet Darcy himself. Both he and Elizabeth are embarrassed, he leaves suddenly, but returns and shows how well-bred and good-mannered he is, even inviting Mr Gardiner to fish in his stream. Darcy tells Elizabeth that he will be joined by Bingley and his sister the next day, and is particularly intent upon introducing his own sister Georgiana to Elizabeth then. Later Elizabeth puts Mrs Gardiner right about the Darcy-Wickham situation.

Commentrary

This chapter contains noteworthy descriptions of the house and some fine natural description as well. Elizabeth is forced to consider that she *might* have been mistress of Pemberley; Mrs Reynolds's account shows Darcy in a completely new light and tends to confirm Darcy's account of Wickham's behaviour. There is a natural control of dialogue, with Elizabeth's consciousness registering all that is said and showing her own feelings being educated the more she hears of Darcy. A fine dramatic stroke is the entrance of Darcy himself, with Elizabeth's shame at being seen there and amazement that Darcy should be so kind and courteous to her – and her friends – and even enquiring after her family. Elizabeth shows her sensitivity throughout this chapter, and it is quite apparent that she is flattered by Darcy's natural goodness to the Gardiners and also by his wish to introduce Georgiana to her. The narrative is balanced between Elizabeth's inner feelings, the drama of meeting Darcy, and some fine outward and inward description.

nor falsely adorned i.e. landscaped.
prospect View.
rattle away Chatter.
distraction i.e. he was not concentrating properly because of his surprise.
discrimination i.e. his seeing them.
strike into Take.
whimsical in his civilities i.e. somewhat unpredictable in his manners.
flaming i.e. superb, outstanding.

Chapter 44

Darcy and his sister call and Bingley soon joins them. Elizabeth takes to Georgiana, and soon sees in her own mind that Bingley is *not* intent on courting her (Georgiana). She also detects something in Bingley which makes her feel that he still has a tenderness for Jane. They are all invited to dine at Pemberley, and Elizabeth examines her own mind with regard to Darcy, feeling gratitude towards him and some shame for her own attitudes in the past.

Commentary

The description of Georgiana and Elizabeth's own observation show Darcy's sister to be a shy but pleasant girl; the Gardiners meanwhile come to the conclusion that Darcy is in love with Elizabeth. The latter's concern for Jane and her close observation of Bingley reinforce her suspicions that Bingley still cares for Jane, and she becomes more and more impressed by Darcy's manners and the consideration he shows for herself and the Gardiners. Elizabeth's state of mind as she is alone is movingly conveyed; she is having to re-think her own attitudes, is conscious of new emotions and, typically, is honest enough to blame herself for her misjudgement of Darcy. The Gardiners have an important functional part in the plot – they determine to return Darcy's call, thus bringing Elizabeth into his company once again.

curricle Two-wheeled open carriage drawn by two horses sisde by side.
livery Badge on the carriage, the uniform of the driver.
untinctured Unflavoured.
acrimony Bitterness.
expedient Appropriate.

Chapter 45

The morning call is made, and Miss Darcy and her companion receive Elizabeth courteously, Mrs Hurst and Miss Bingley barely acknowledging her. Meanwhile Darcy is talking to Mr Gardiner and some friends by the river, but he soon enters; Georgiana's conversation improves at this. Miss Bingley's talk of the militia aimed at embarrassing Elizabeth, in fact leaves Georgiana much embarrassed. Seeking to provoke Darcy by remarking on Elizabeth's appearance, Miss Bingley only succeeds in drawing from Darcy personal praise of Elizabeth's beauty.

Commentary

Contrast between Elizabeth – somewhat on edge in waiting for Darcy's appearance – Miss Bingley, all jealousy and ill-breeding – and Georgiana, shy, diffident but anxious to please her brother by playing the hostess when he does appear. The irony plays over the fact that in seeking to embarrass Elizabeth by mentioning the militia Miss Bingley unwittingly upsets Georgiana for fear she should mention Wickham. Georgiana is loyal to Darcy in refusing to join in Miss Bingley's criticism of Elizabeth when the latter leaves, and Miss Bingley gets what she deserves when, seeking to undermine Elizabeth with Darcy, she hears him praise her 'as one of the handsomest women of my acquaintance'.

corps Militia, regiment.

Chapter 46

Elizabeth receives two letters from Jane on the same morning, one of which has been wrongly addressed. Her delight changes to distress as she learns that Lydia has eloped with Wickham. It is thought that the pair may be in London. When Darcy enters he sees how upset Elizabeth is. The Gardiners are sent for, and Elizabeth through her tears tells Darcy what news she has just received of Lydia and Wickham. Darcy assures her that he will keep the matter secret, seems to be absorbed, and when the Gardiners arrive, they and Elizabeth set out for Longbourn.

Commentary

Note once more the device of the letter to convey information and heighten the dramatic situation. Narrative tension is raised by the speculation over Lydia and Wickham and their action, and note that the style in which the letter is written reflects the disturbance, the movement, the changes, which have suddenly occurred. The atmosphere between Elizabeth and Darcy is charged with her concern for what has happened and his obvious if unexpressed love for her. Note also how Elizabeth blames herself for not speaking out about Wickham after Darcy had told her what he knew of him. The tension is maintained at the end of the chapter by the sudden departure for Longbourn, with the reader, as well as Elizabeth and the Gardiners, on tenterhooks to learn more.

the direction i.e. address.
disinterested i.e. the implication is that he must love Lydia, since she has no money of her own.
hackney-coach Hired carriage.
palliation Diminishing.
varieties Variations.
infamy Disgraceful conduct.
deranged Worried, upset.
actuated Motivated.

Chapter 47

Elizabeth reveals her knowledge of Wickham's previous behaviour to her aunt and uncle on their way to Longbourn. Jane and Elizabeth are reunited, Mr Bennet has gone to

London, and the practical Mr Gardiner decides to follow him. Mrs Bennet has collapsed and Jane has assumed responsibility for the household despite the strain, Mary falls back on her moral reflections. Elizabeth gets more details of the elopement from Jane, who shows her Lydia's letter to Mrs Forster, which is thoughtless and brash in its expressions.

Commentary

Mr Gardiner shows his common sense and optimism, but Elizabeth is the focus of the contemporary conventional sexual morality which would have been shocked at Lydia's and Wickham's pre-marital relations. Elizabeth has the character to admit that she did not forewarn Lydia about Wickham, though it would probably have made little difference. There is some neat authorial irony on 'this interesting subject', some genuine comedy despite the seriousness of the situation in Mrs Bennet's lamentations and fears that Mr Bennet will fight Wickham. Mary has her prepared pomposity to contribute, Mr Gardiner his practicality in going to town to seek out Mr Bennet. Kitty reveals her duplicity, for Lydia had hinted what she was going to do. Lydia's note to Mrs Forster is a masterpiece of brash insensitivity, selfishness, indulgence, superficiality and a certain *pride* in being what she is – a coquette determined on marriage. She also believes she has done rather better than her sisters in securing Wickham. Elizabeth's edginess is shown in the way she receives the news that Lady Lucas has called with her condolences.

susceptibility to her feelings i.e. encouraged herself by thinking of nothing (but the officers).
directions Instructions.
sanguine Optimistic.
moral extractions i.e. deductions from their present situation on which she could make generalized moral conclusions.
postilions i.e. riders, drivers of coach-horses.

Chapter 48

Wickham's character is blackened in Meryton, Mr Gardiner goes to London, and Mr Collins writes an extraordinary letter of 'sympathy' about Lydia's elopement which contains no Christian charity and the much-quoted 'The death of your daughter would have been a blessing in comparison of this'. Wickham has left gambling debts at Brighton. Mr Bennet, unsuccessful in his search for the lovers, returns to Longbourn as Mrs Gardiner and the children leave. Mr Bennet blames himself for not taking Elizabeth's advice about sending Lydia to Brighton, and wittily applies his new caution to Kitty.

Commentary

This fine chapter contains ironic comments on the fickleness of society (its change of heart over Wickham – whose character is further blackened by the stigma of gambling), the general ineptitude of Mr Bennet and the hypocrisy of Mr Collins. The letter – note the use of the letter again – written by a Christian clergyman reflects a totally unchristian attitude. It is a satire, I feel, on the excessive lip-service paid to convention – with the self-congratulatory addition that Mr Collins feels himself fortunate not to have married into the Bennet family. Mrs Gardiner continues to speculate upon Elizabeth's feelings for Darcy, and Elizabeth acknowledges to herself that she would have found Lydia's behaviour more acceptable had she not known Darcy. Mr Bennet shows character and honesty in confessing himself in error to Elizabeth, but his teasing of Kitty reveals him in a typical, languidly witty mood.

dilatory i.e. casual, unreliable.
pleasing intelligence Good news.
The death of your daughter . . . The key to Mr Collins's character – he must only be associated with what is eminently respectable.
throw off your unworthy child . . . A reinforcement of the above statement and comment.
powdering gown Loose garment to protect the clothes while a man had his head powdered.
review Military parade.

Chapter 49

Mr Gardiner writes to Mr Bennet that he has traced the lovers, who are willing to be married according to the arrangements made by Mr Gardiner on Mr Bennet's account – £100 per annum to be given to Lydia while Mr Bennet is alive, and also her equal share of the £5000 settled on the Bennet children by their father. It occurs to Mr Bennet that someone has paid Wickham money to agree to this, and he suspects Mr Gardiner of doing so. Mrs Bennet ceases to be an invalid, praises her kind brother, and triumphs in Lydia's being married at sixteen.

Commentary

The now familiar device of the letter conveys the important news, but notice Mr Bennet's sharpness – and honesty – in recognizing, and speaking openly about the fact that some inducement must have been offered to Wickham. Jane, as always, sees the good she wants to see in Wickham, thinking that he is genuinely fond of Lydia, and Elizabeth has the practicality to want to know what Wickham's debts are in order to find out what Mr Gardiner had had to pay out. Mrs Bennet's reactions are predictable and totally within character – her quick recovery stimulated by the news of the impending marriage, which is in a sense a triumph for her, since she has always set out to marry off her daughters.

transports i.e. expressions of happiness.

Chapter 50

Mr Bennet wishes that he had saved money earlier in life, though he stands to lose very little money from what he believes to be Mr Gardiner's generous payment. Mrs Bennet now proceeds to organize possible houses in the neighbourhood for Lydia and Wickham. Mr Bennet at first says he won't receive Lydia and Wickham into the family home, and Elizabeth ponders on how well Darcy would have suited her. Mr Gardiner writes to say that Wickham has decided to quit the militia and join the regulars, being posted to serve in the North. This allows Mr Bennet to consent to their coming home before they go.

Commentary

Mr Bennet shows in his reactions to Mr Gardiner's generosity an awareness at last of his own shortcomings. Mrs Bennet's transition with 'No sentiment of shame' continues until she realizes that Mr Bennet will not contribute towards Lydia's trousseau.

But by far the most moving part of this chapter is Elizabeth's awakening recognition of her family's lack of merit and of Darcy's particular marks of worth. It leads her to be humbled, grieved, repentant. Again a letter brings important news – that Wickham has been purchased a commission in the regulars, and that he and Lydia are to go north.

cutting off the entail i.e. purchasing the family's succession.
approbation Agreement.
gave a damp Put down.
connubial felicity Marital happiness.

Revision questions on Chapters 41–50

1 Compare and contrast the various reactions of the Bennet family to Lydia's going to Brighton.

2 In what ways does Elizabeth find her knowledge of Darcy expanding and her views changing during and after her visit to Pemberley?

3 Write an essay on Jane Austen's use of the letter in some or any of these chapters.

4 In what ways does Jane Austen raise dramatic expectation in any *two* chapters here?

5 Compare and contrast Mr Bennet and Mr Gardiner.

Chapter 51

Lydia, full of herself, arrives with Wickham, delighted and boastful of her married status. Mrs Bennet is equally exuberant about welcoming her one married daughter, ill-breeding characterizing their exchanges. Lydia hardly stops talking, wishes to visit all and sundry, but Elizabeth soon observes that Wickham's 'affection' for Lydia is not as great as Lydia's for him. Lydia lets slip that Darcy was present at her marriage, something she had been told to keep secret, and Elizabeth is so intrigued that she writes to Mrs Gardiner about the matter.

Commentary

Lydia as we should expect, Wickham smooth and in Elizabeth's eyes impudent, Mr Bennet austere, Mrs Bennet garrulous; Lydia promises to try to get husbands for her sisters, but her rattling leads to the plot revelation that it was Darcy who accompanied Wickham to his wedding. Thus the chapter ends on a high note of expectation as Elizabeth writes to Mrs Gardiner.

Chapter 52

Mrs Gardiner's reply reveals Darcy's major role in events. He provided the money which enabled Lydia and Wickham to marry, having first found where they were living. He blamed himself for making Wickham's worthlessness sufficiently well-known. Wickham originally had no intention of marrying, but Darcy had bought him a commission in the regulars and also provided £1000 for Lydia's dowry. Mrs Gardiner hints in the letters that she is convinced that Darcy's real motive in doing all this is his interest in Elizabeth. He has refused to let his name be revealed in connection with this affair, but Mrs Gardiner is sure that one day Elizabeth will be mistress of Pemberley. Elizabeth's feelings are thrown into a tumult by all this and, shortly afterwards, she is joined by Wickham of all people. Elizabeth spars with him, finds him deceitful as usual, and succeeds in making him understand that she knows what he is doing.

Commentary

Once more the letter is used as plot device, and here as much more, since we see Darcy's sensitivity as well as his generosity and learn, as the Gardiners know, that it is all for Elizabeth. Mr Gardiner is irked by the fact that he will get the public credit for Darcy's private generosity; Lydia is silly and selfish, Wickham opportunist and unscrupulous. Elizabeth is delighted that the Gardiners appreciate Darcy but also appreciates the awkward situation she now finds herself in – surely Darcy could never demean himself by proposing again and becoming Wickham's brother-in-law! The last part of the chapter is given over to a delightful exchange, as Wickham tries to reestablish himself with Elizabeth and is counter-attacked with gentle but complete effect every time he tries a lie and suggests an innuendo.

racked Tormented.
answerable for the event Responsible for the outcome.
another interest i.e. in Elizabeth.
the most trying age Elizabeth is being heavily sarcastic – the most
   trying age would be when Georgiana nearly eloped with Wickham.
repine Complain.

Chapter 53

Lydia and Wickham leave and the Bennets learn that Netherfield is to be reoccupied. Mr Bennet will not be persuaded to call
on Bingley, but Bingley and Darcy soon call at Longbourn.
Elizabeth – and Darcy – are both embarrassed, and this is added
to by the insensitive way in which Lydia's marriage is spoken of.
Elizabeth tries to forget this by noticing how well Jane and
Bingley are getting on. As they leave Mrs Bennet invites them
both to dine at Longbourn.

Commentary

Mr Bennet indulges his irony at the expense of Wickham – 'He
simpers, and smirks, and makes love to us all' – and Mrs Bennet
her expectations at the return of Wickham. There is of course
some irony present in the fact that Elizabeth has not shown Jane
Mrs Gardiner's letter which reveals Darcy's goodness on her
family's behalf, and this adds to the tension when Darcy appears,
and probably accounts for his own reserved behaviour. Mrs
Bennet's 'cold and ceremonious' behaviour to Darcy only height-
ens the irony, as does the embarrassingly complacent account of
the report of Lydia's marriage as if it were a great social success.
The latter is virtually ignored by Mrs Bennet's officious attentions to Mr Bingley.

in the fidgets Restless.
unequal Unpredictable.
coveys Flocks of birds.

Chapter 54

Elizabeth broods on Darcy's behaviour. The dinner party on the
following Tuesday finds Jane and Bingley getting on well, Darcy
and Elizabeth placed at a distance. During the evening there is

hardly an opportunity for conversation, and although the family generally think that the party has passed off well, Elizabeth is dissatisfied. She has the spirit, however, to tease Jane about her renewed friendship with Bingley.

Commentary

This is a study in the dissatisfaction of the main lovers Elizabeth and Darcy, neither of whom knows quite how to approach the other, and the gradual coming together of the secondary pair Jane and Bingley. Darcy shows his pride and reserve (and his forbearance in tolerating the odious Mrs Bennet) and we note again the sensitivity of Darcy and Elizabeth each in their separate ways not knowing how to effect what they most want – the company of the other.

consequence Outcome.

Chapter 55

Bingley visits Longbourn again, and Mrs Bennet contrives to leave him alone with Jane. She is unsuccessful, but the next day he goes shooting with Mr Bennet, returns to dinner, and, Mrs Bennet this time having managed things successfully, is left to talk to Jane. When Elizabeth enters the room, she learns that her sister and Bingley are engaged. There is general delight, Mrs Bennet in her 'transports' proclaiming Jane her 'favourite child'. Elizabeth learns from Jane that Bingley confesses to having loved her earlier; but Bingley does not reveal the influence of Darcy in his affairs, and nor does Elizabeth. The Bennets are now acclaimed by the local gossip where before they were damned over Lydia's elopement with Wickham.

Commentary

This chapter is a mixture of comedy, romance and reaction. The comedy lies in Mrs Bennet's contrivances to get the lovers together – her 'winking' perhaps the most grotesque part of it – the romance is Jane's revelation of her happiness, but note also her concern to let her mother know from the best possible motives. The reaction is Elizabeth's, that despite Darcy's earlier officiousness and Miss Bingley's actions they have reached 'the happiest, wisest, most reasonable end!' Even Mr Bennet is happy, if that is not too strong a word.

circumspection Caution.
complying Easy-going, relaxed.

Chapter 56

Lady Catherine calls at Longbourn, disdains Mrs Bennet, and wishes to speak to Elizabeth in the garden. She launches a verbal attack on Elizabeth by asking her if she is engaged to Darcy; Elizabeth parries the initial and following attacks, but refuses to give a guarantee with regard to Darcy though she does admit that they are not engaged. Lady Catherine leaves haughtily, but Mrs Bennet is of course flattered by the visit.

Commentary

This is one of the finest chapters in the novel, with Elizabeth's spirit – and courage – counteracting Lady Catherine at every turn of that obstinate woman's pride and prejudice. Lady Catherine emerges as the complete snob, but here her condescension does not work – she meets a young girl who has seen her dominate her own territory but now, on the Longbourn territory, finds an independent view is equal to her ladyship's impertinent pretensions. Elizabeth will not be bullied, and the truth to life of the dialogue is one of the most impressive things about this chapter, though Lady Catherine's tone occasionally descends into caricature. The scene is dramatic, emotional, vivid; the last irony is Mrs Bennet's misunderstanding of the visit and her own snobbery in having entertained a lady of rank. She has no inkling of what has happened and, such is Jane Austen's art, no inkling of what is to come.

interest i.e. it is in Elizabeth's interest to refuse Darcy because his family and all connected with them will ignore her.
importuned i.e. pestered.

Chapter 57

Elizabeth is much put out by what has happened, and even feels that Lady Catherine will influence Darcy; Mr Bennet meanwhile has received a letter from Mr Collins telling him of the rumour of an engagement between Elizabeth and Darcy and congratulating him on the hushing up of the Lydia-Wickham affair. Elizabeth, on learning the contents of the letter, has to react as her father expects, by pretending to be amused by it.

Commentary

Another chapter in which there is a neat balance struck between the irony of Mr Bennet not knowing Elizabeth's real feelings, her own examination of her heart and her reactions after the distressing scene with Lady Catherine, and yet another letter which moves the plot forward by coupling the names of Elizabeth and Darcy. Mr Bennet hugely enjoys the joke of Mr Collins's Christian charity *and* the idea that there could ever be serious feeling between Elizabeth and the man she apparently dislikes so much, Darcy.

The discomposure of spirits i.e. depression.
sagacity Wisdom and insight.
diverted Amused.

Chapter 58

While walking with Darcy, Elizabeth tells him how grateful she is both on her own and her family's account for all he has done for Lydia. He approaches the subject of his feelings for her, and she tells him that hers have changed towards him since he proposed to her the previous April. Their happiness is almost too great for words, but nevertheless they have a long conversation which clears all misunderstandings between them.

Commentary

This is a moving chapter, in which both Darcy and Elizabeth are stripped of their pride and their prejudice. They are honest in their expressions, Darcy revealing a humility and generosity which complements Elizabeth's spirit. Even the description of their silence after the acknowledgement of their feelings is superbly done – the reserved man quiet in his delight, Elizabeth too full of happiness for words. Both are recognizing the development in their feelings, the fact that they have learned that their 'first impressions' were wrong. Perhaps the most moving acknowledgement is Darcy's confession of his not telling Bingley that Jane had been in town during the previous winter.

Chapter 59

Elizabeth confides her happiness to Jane, who of course initially doubts that she can be in love with Darcy. Mrs Bennet arranges a walk, apologizing for throwing Darcy and Elizabeth together since she knows that Elizabeth cannot stand him. In the evening Darcy goes into the library to make his formal proposal for Elizabeth to Mr Bennet; the latter sends for Elizabeth, is amazed to find that she cares for Darcy, and even more amazed that Darcy has managed Lydia's affairs both practically and financially. On hearing the news, Mrs Bennet changes her mind about Darcy and about her favourite daughter – Lizzy has made the most advantageous match and without her mother's help!

Commentary

The confidences between Jane and Elizabeth are moving and convincing, with Elizabeth's sense of humour playing over all. There is a neatly ironic section in which Mrs Bennet unwittingly provides the privacy which the lovers wish for by sending them on a walk together. Mr Bennet shows his real concern for Lizzie, and their exchange and her revelations about Darcy are poignant with the often unvoiced love between father and daughter, though Mr Bennet cannot avoid a touch of whimsy – 'If any young men come for Mary or Kitty, send them in, for I am quite at leisure.' Mrs Bennet predictably nearly goes 'distracted' but is in awe of her future son-in-law; her husband drily comments that perhaps Wickham is his favourite son-in-law.

Chapter 60

A delightful interchange between Elizabeth and Darcy in which they discuss their initial prejudices and their subsequent love for each other. Elizabeth writes the news of her engagement to Mrs Gardiner, and Mr Bennet feels moved to do the same briefly to Mr Collins, urging him to console Lady Catherine as best he can. The Collinses arrive however, since Charlotte wishes to see Elizabeth (and to escape Lady Catherine's mood); Darcy has to endure the obsequiousness of Mr Collins, as well as the vulgarity of Mrs Philips. Elizabeth contemplates the future away from her family with some degree of serenity.

Commentary

Elizabeth is playful and frank with Darcy, who reveals that Lady Catherine's actions have been material in persuading him that there was hope in his proposing to Elizabeth again. Again the device of letters – Elizabeth's to Mrs Gardiner, Darcy's to Lady Catherine and Mr Bennet's to Mr Collins – is used to convey the important news. There is pathos in the retreat of the Collinses to Lucas Lodge, since they have to go back to live with Lady Catherine sooner or later. Yet another letter, this time from Georgiana, though not printed in the text, contains all her joyfulness of spirit in her brother's forthcoming marriage.

Chapter 61

All is rounded off. Mr Bennet misses Elizabeth, but visits Pemberley from time to time and Bingley and Jane buy an estate near the Darcys. Lydia importunes Elizabeth for money and gets some, though she and Wickham are not happy. Kitty improves, Miss Bingley reforms her views and, after some time there is a part reconciliation between Darcy and his aunt. Georgiana and Elizabeth become great friends. Mrs Bennet is left largely to Mary's company, and that young lady therefore has to go into society.

Commentary

We note the author's moral tone through to the end. Though Miss Bingley reforms, Lydia continues irresponsible. Mr Bennet, as to be expected, visits Pemberley when 'least expected'. The whole chapter is a neat index to the lives we have followed.

Revision questions on Chapters 51–61

1 Write a character sketch of Lydia as she appears to the reader on her return to Longbourn.

2 How important is the part played by Darcy in the settling of the Lydia-Wickham affair, and what effect does it have on the plot of the novel?

3 Describe the various reactions to the engagement of Darcy and Elizabeth, with particular reference to the members of the Bennet family.

4 By a close look at the dialogue in any one or two scenes, say whether you think Elizabeth and Darcy are suited to one another and why.

5 Write an account of the exchange between Elizabeth and Lady Catherine de Bourgh.

6 Indicate the part played by letters in these final chapters.

Jane Austen's art in *Pride and Prejudice*
The characters

Elizabeth

I hope I never ridicule what is wise and good.

Elizabeth is one of the outstanding heroines of fiction. She is guilty of pride and prejudice, but she learns from her mistakes, embraces humility on occasions, and has great reserves of spirit and strength. She has no cloying goodness, rather a capacity for judgement and sympathy which is winning because it is frank, open and discerning. She is devoted to her sister Jane, who can see no wrong in anybody; she is aware of her family's faults, yet obedient to her mother's instructions, thus putting herself in the way of being proposed to by Mr Collins, a man she abhors for his sycophantic and pompous attitude. Elizabeth is moved by her heart, responding (misguidedly) to Wickham's account of his victimization at the hands of Darcy, and to Jane's illness while she is staying at Netherfield. Her independence of character, her sense of what is right, is shown in her reasoning with her father not to let Lydia go to Brighton; if he had listened, the affair with Wickham would certainly not have occurred.

Elizabeth is the moral pivot of the novel. It is through her eyes that we largely watch events as they occur, and it is to her judgement that we look. When she overhears Darcy describe her as 'tolerable' we are told that she has no 'cordial' feelings for that gentleman, but she 'told the story with great spirit among her friends; for she had a lively, playful disposition, which delighted in anything ridiculous' (p. 7). She fosters Jane's liking for Bingley (note that no mercenary considerations are involved) but is cautious about Miss Bingley and Mrs Hurst, and later sees through them completely. She exchanges confidences with her friend Charlotte Lucas, plays and sings but without affectation, has the courage to refuse to dance with Darcy, and resists the pursuit of officers in which Lydia and Kitty indulge. Her visit to Jane shows her capacity to flout convention, and it also shows her inherent health and physical attraction, something we should notice since it conditions Darcy's responses to her. Her tolerance is shown in her sensing that she may have misjudged

Miss Bingley and Mrs Hurst, but in fact her 'first impressions' are right, and she soon becomes aware of Miss Bingley's designs on Darcy. She trembles 'lest her mother should be exposing herself again' (Chapter 9, p. 33), for Elizabeth is well-bred without being snobbish, and is conscious of correct behaviour and of her own family's vulgarity (with the exception of Jane and her father).

Elizabeth is very observant, but she is also clear-sighted in her judgements, seeing from his letter that the words are the man in the case of Mr Collins. Before his proposal to her, however, Elizabeth is attracted to Wickham. It is not until much later — and this is the measure of her judgement and self-examination — that she realizes that in talking to her so freely shortly after their meeting Wickham had been at best indiscreet, at worst wicked. Her initial response to Wickham shows a degree of impetuosity, but remember that she *wants* to think ill of Darcy because of his pride. She even says of Wickham 'there was truth in his looks' (Chapter 17, p. 64). She is naturally disappointed when Wickham does not attend the ball. Her exchanges with Darcy there only confirm her opinion of him, and she responds to Miss Bingley's account of Wickham with spirit and forthrightness, calling that unpleasant woman an 'Insolent girl' (Chapter 18, p. 72) to herself.

Elizabeth is resilient and has the verbal wit required to take on the rather humourless Darcy. It is the same wit she employs (though in a kindly manner) on her sister Jane when she rallies her about her goodness. Her rightness of feeling is apparent throughout the novel, for she always behaves well and with discretion. On learning that Charlotte is to marry Mr Collins, she quickly recovers her own wonder and sublimates it, but it is one of the few occasions when she allows her feelings to get the better of her. Quite typically, her 'Impossible' becomes generous acceptance of her friend's position, and the mark of her friendship is shown in her undertaking the visit to Charlotte and Mr Collins, though she knows that the latter will be all condescension. Elizabeth has the exquisite sensitivity to pity her friend and not show it.

At Rosings Elizabeth is admirable, riding the worst verbal excesses, ill-breeding and domination of Lady Catherine by her own quiet honesty and yet firmness of attitude. She is secretly amused at the idea of Darcy being interested in Lady Anne, for a time impressionable enough to feel that Colonel Fitzwilliam might be attracted to *her*, and then, after her frequent casual meetings with Darcy in the Park, is at first overcome and then made angry by his proposal. But she finds the spirit to reply and reject in no uncertain terms, and in doing so she shows her love for her sister – whom she believes wronged by Darcy – and her lack of judgement in dragging what she believes is the truth about Wickham and Darcy into that reply. Again the measure of her self-analysis, the integrity which makes her look and think again and then revise, is shown in her careful readings of Darcy's letter. When they meet again at Pemberley she realizes how wrong she has been, and she begins to appraise the man for what he is as her own feelings take on the aspect of love.

Back with her family she recognizes the truth of Darcy's appraisal of her mother and sisters. At Pemberley she is conscious of Darcy's inherent good-breeding, is proud of her uncle, and considerate to the shy and uncertain though likeable Georgiana. Despite the past, she takes pleasure in renewing her acquaintance with Bingley, seeking for some indication from him that he still feels for her sister. She is aware that Darcy is still interested in her, and comes to feel the compliment of his asking her to marry him. That feeling soon gives way to one of dependence; after reading Jane's letter about the elopement of Lydia and Wickham, Elizabeth is so overcome with shock as to break down before Darcy. That shock is partly owing to her own feeling of guilt, since she had known what Wickham was like but had not warned Mr Bennet or Lydia. She feels that she has now lost Darcy for ever, but her immediate concern is to be at home with her family, for Elizabeth's is essentially a loyal character. That loyalty does not prevent her from condemning Lydia or from listening with amazement to the inappropriate moralizing of her sister Mary.

We note that in this crisis Mr Gardiner places some reliance on Elizabeth's judgement, while her father acknowledges her 'greatness of mind' (Chapter 48, p. 221) in the advice she gave him – and which he disregarded – over Lydia going to Brighton. Like the others, she jumps to the conclusion that Mr Gardiner bought Wickham and is sickened to find her mother indulging in transports of self-congratulation now that Lydia is to be married. Disgusted by Lydia's own lack of conscience about what she has done, she yet learns from her that Darcy was present at the wedding. She quickly discovers from her aunt the truth of what happened. From then on, her own love deepens as she realizes what Darcy has done for her and her family – 'Her heart did whisper that he had done it for her' (Chapter 52, p. 241). Her thoughts are filled with feelings for him and, soon afterwards, accosted by her brother-in-law Wickham, she leaves him in no doubt that she knows what he is and what he has done.

But before the lovers come together Elizabeth fights a major battle, and this after the engagement of Jane and Bingley is known. In the commentary to Chapter 56 I have already indicated that the scene between Lady Catherine and Elizabeth is one of the finest in the novel. Though Elizabeth is caught off her guard, her resilience, good breeding, good sense and natural ability to command words and argument serve to put down the pretentious interference of Lady Catherine. A mark of her triumph is her independence – '*You* may ask questions which *I* shall not choose to answer' (Chapter 56, p. 262) and a brilliant recourse to sarcasm – 'These are heavy misfortunes . . . But the wife of Mr Darcy must have such extraordinary sources of happiness necessarily attached to her situation, that she could, upon the whole, have no cause to repine' (p. 263). By the simple expedient of demonstrating her right to choose Elizabeth puts down the insufferable snobbery of Lady Catherine.

With no ulterior motive than the wish to acknowledge his generosity, Elizabeth thanks Darcy for what he has done; from then on their love for each other can no longer be hidden, and the effects on the family, from Jane to Mr Bennet to Mrs Bennet, and the changes these occasion in their attitudes towards the proud man they thought Elizabeth disliked, are part of a rich fabric of comedy. Elizabeth's own playfulness is a nice contrast to Darcy's seriousness; they complement each other now that each has overcome the strength of first impressions and their own pride and prejudice.

Darcy

He was at the same time haughty, reserved, and fastidious, and his manners, though well bred, were not inviting.

It is obvious from the beginning that Darcy, despite himself, is attracted to Elizabeth, so much so that he offers to dance with her although he dislikes dancing. Darcy's reticence and pride conceal sensitivity and capacity for action, but he responds to the baiting of Miss Bingley by admitting that he has been 'meditating on the very great pleasure which a pair of fine eyes in the face of a pretty woman can bestow' (Chapter 6, p. 19). His response when Elizabeth walks over to Netherfield to see Jane shows that he is sexually attracted to her, though the reticence which the conventions of Jane Austen's times demanded does not allow any full expression apart from the fact that he finds Elizabeth's eyes 'brightened'.

Constantly faced with Miss Bingley's attentions, Darcy has the character and insight to see through her and to put her in her place. His pride is shown in his tolerating, and that is all, the attentions of Sir William Lucas, the obsequiousness of Mr Collins and, of course, enduring the vulgarity of Mrs Bennet and her younger daughters. His exchanges with Elizabeth show an active mind, though perhaps not equal to the vivacity of her humour and the quickness of her repartee. He has, like Elizabeth, a store of common-sense wisdom, as when he observes 'Nothing is more deceitful . . . than the appearance of humility' (Chapter 10, p. 35). His dignity is often threatened by Elizabeth's vivacity, but he smiles quietly in response to her scoring off him.

The remarkable thing in Jane Austen's presentation of Darcy is that he is shown in two ways – the disagreeable, proud and withdrawn man at Netherfield who arouses hostility and who would apparently confirm Wickham's accounts of him. That is the first; the second is his housekeeper's reports of him at Pemberley, and his conduct to Elizabeth and the Gardiners when he meets them. In between this is his proposal to Elizabeth, which shows him to be proud and condescending but at the same time passionate in his feelings. He has fought against them but, to his credit, feelings have won, and when he is castigated over Wickham his pride, since he feels the injustice of Elizabeth's charges, causes him to write a letter which is clear, honest, and which Elizabeth cannot refute. Even this letter ends with a blessing, so that we know at once that Darcy is not the hard man he appears to so many.

Darcy is generous, to his tenants, to the poor, to his sister and even to Wickham, both before the Lydia affair and during it. He sinks his pride, he learns humility. Like Elizabeth, he is a developing character. Concerned for Elizabeth's distress on account of the Lydia-Wickham elopement, he puts things right (if they ever can be) by devoting his time, energy, and indeed money to relieving the distress of Elizabeth and her family. We know that he is doing it out of love for Elizabeth, but he is never reduced to romantic caricature by what he does. His keeping his part secret is an instance of nobility of character – he does not seek to recommend himself to Elizabeth by what he has done, but merely to bring about the best possible result from the unhappy affair. We remember his kindness to his sister Georgiana and his protection of her, and here again – in preventing *her* elopement with Wickham – he shows that he is capable of quick positive action to avoid disaster.

Darcy is a good judge of character and his judgement of Bingley is sound. However, he has no insight into the feelings of Jane. He sees through the obvious pretensions of people like Sir William Lucas and Mr Collins, and sets a great premium on breeding though he is himself rude on occasions. This rudeness may spring from two causes – an inability to suffer fools or bores and a reticence or reserve which makes it difficult for him to sustain a part in society. He *is* proud, well aware of his status in relation to Elizabeth, and, unwisely, letting her know it in his proposal. But he learns, and it is this capacity which endears him to us. His services to the Bennet family are great, though they do not know it at once, and his admission that he did not tell Bingley that Jane was in London shows that he is able to admit error and embrace humility. This is a major moral step forward for the man who saw no one worthy of his attention at the Netherfield ball.

It is Elizabeth's rejection of him which, I suppose, brings him to reconsider his position and makes him tell her so much more in the letter than he could ever speak. He has to explain himself, but he does so with remarkable fluency and directness; it is the mark of the man that he should tell the woman he loves, who has rejected him, so much by way of explanation in this intimate manner. We must remember that his world – his image of himself – has been shattered by that rejection. His *pride* did not allow him to think that Elizabeth could turn him down. The changes in Darcy are not so remarkable as they appear; his housekeeper's account to Elizabeth and the Gardiners shows the real pattern of his life, his domestic life, with the care of his sister and his undoubted goodness to her and all those with whom he comes into contact in the neighbourhood. This is the real Darcy. The other Darcy is the one who *appears* at Netherfield and doesn't much like what he sees – a woman trying to manipulate her daughter into marriage, much vulgar and ostentatious behaviour, and judges all – Elizabeth apart – severely. Darcy is in error, but we recall Elizabeth's visit to Netherfield and realize that Darcy is consistent – he has little time for the display of Miss Bingley, puts her in her place once or twice, and does not entertain any gossip. Darcy is a study in psychological consistency, as is Elizabeth. They complement each other admirably; the wit and vivacity come from her, but he has some sense of humour, as we see from his exchanges with her, and a good and rational command of language, though he is not verbose. Darcy represents the reality, convincing reality, of change, but his moral stance is consistent throughout. He has to shift his pride and his prejudice, but the shifts are real, acknowledged, honest, for Darcy is a man of moral rectitude and integrity.

Jane

All loveliness and goodness – her understanding excellent, her mind improved and her manners captivating.

At first sight Jane may appear somewhat cloying, since she never thinks ill of anybody, and is almost teased on occasions by Elizabeth for thinking so naively. It is obvious that when Jane meets Bingley she falls immediately in love, though she herself would not admit this and in fact thinks of him, after he has left for London, as one of the most pleasant men of her acquaintance. Jane is a study in reticence and goodness, and she does not cloy because we accept her suffering, realizing that her essential goodness of nature renders her vulnerable. Not only does she respond to Bingley she also responds to his sisters, mistaking their superficiality for sincerity, their sympathetic interest for friendship. Her education is in the hard school of life, for when she goes to London and sees Miss Bingley she realizes that the latter has no wish for her company. Later of course she comes to know that Bingley has been got away from Netherfield by their wish (and of course by Darcy too) but even then she expresses no ill-will against them. She lacks Elizabeth's social personality, verve and wit, but she is capable of taking up a firm position and sticking to it. She is very beautiful – even Darcy acknowledges this – but it is the kind of beauty which excites admiration rather than jealousy; whereas we get a clear impression of Elizabeth's sex appeal, we get no idea of any physicality in Jane.

Jane tries, because of her essentially noble and generous nature, to make the best of everything that happens. She reacts generously to Charlotte Lucas's marriage to Mr Collins, for although she is surprised she is more concerned for their happiness than anything else. She is constantly seen or reported as being out of 'spirits', an indication of her love for Bingley which she will not outwardly acknowledge. When she and Elizabeth are reunited and Elizabeth tells her of Darcy's proposal, she is able to express sadness over the revelation of Wickham's past behaviour, yet at the same time she tells Elizabeth that 'I never thought Mr Darcy so deficient in the *appearance* of it [goodness] as you used to do' (Chapter 40, p.167). She even counsels silence on Wickham's guilt to Elizabeth, and this reveals her cautious nature, for if Elizabeth had revealed it, Lydia might have been saved.

Jane has an important function in the plot of *Pride and Prejudice*. While Elizabeth tastes the joys of Pemberley and Darcy's courtesy and obvious love, Jane's letters reveal the family crisis and promote her sister's immediate return. She writes with graphic immediacy, and has the insight to trust to her uncle's practicality of action. Jane holds the fort at home, her sympathetic nature even finding redeeming features in the crisis, praising the behaviour of Colonel Forster and finding Lady Lucas's visits kind rather than inquisitive. She responds positively to the arrival of the Gardiners, 'welcomed and thanked them both, with alternate smiles and tears' (Chapter 47, p. 211). To Elizabeth she appears pale, and it is obvious that the strain has taken its toll.

The news of Bingley's return exposes Jane's sensitivity – 'Not that I am afraid of *myself*, but I dread other people's remarks' (Chapter 53, p. 245). She has only in fact to dread her mother's. When she becomes engaged to Bingley she says 'I do not deserve it' (Chapter 55, p. 256), and she accepts his love and her own happiness with the humility and gratitude which we should expect. She also speaks of her happiness as giving so much pleasure to her family. This is Jane – she is considerate, kind, selfless (sometimes too much so), confiding in Elizabeth but storing her inner feelings and suffering decline accordingly. Yet she takes responsibility in the crisis because, like her sister Elizabeth, she has a moral core of integrity which makes right action and reaction the bases for living.

Mr Bennet

So odd a mixture of quick parts, sarcastic humour, reserve, and caprice, that the experience of three and twenty years had been insufficient to make his wife understand his character.

The Bennet marriage is a study, and a subtle one, of incompatibility between husband and wife which has grown up over a number of years. Mr Bennet has a dry wit, he 'sends up' his wife without her knowing it, and understands her nature and the nature of each of his daughters. In effect, Mr Bennet has abnegated parental responsibility largely by withdrawing into the library in order to avoid his wife's social demands and her nerves, as well as the chatter of his younger daughters. He teases Mary about her capacity for deep reflection based on her reading, and considers Kitty and Lydia two of the silliest girls in the country, but he has a marked preference for Elizabeth, since her intelligence and wit are complementary to his own. He delights in springing a surprise, as he shows when he calls on Bingley, only revealing this after he has done so. His sense of humour, however, conceals a basic indolence and dislike to society, and consequently a crisis finds him wanting. He refuses to listen to Elizabeth when she counsels him not to let Lydia go to Brighton, though he has the grace to acknowledge his error later. He is largely ineffectual in his efforts over the Lydia situation, and all is left to the competence of Mr Gardiner and the generous assumption of responsibility in Darcy. He has some of the finest phrases in the novel. Again we note his delight in the exercise of his humour when he tells Elizabeth:

An unhappy alternative is before you, Elizabeth. From this day you must be a stranger to one of your parents. Your mother will never see you again if you do *not* marry Mr Collins, and I will never see you again if you *do*. (Chapter 20, p. 85).

He takes the Collins marriage in his stride, but when Lydia's crisis arrives, he does what he can to remedy the situation and virtually acknowledges to Elizabeth that he has been waiving his responsibilities over his daughters for years. He tells Kitty that 'I have at last learnt to be cautious' (Chapter 48, p. 221) and he also wishes that he had laid aside an annual sum for his daughters instead of spending his income. But his whimsicality does not desert him. At first forbidding Lydia and Wickham the house, he gives way and allows them to visit; with proposals for Jane and Elizabeth already made, he observes that if any young men call for Kitty and Mary they are to be shown straight into his room. Yet even here we see the depth at which Jane Austen is working on character; when Darcy proposes for Elizabeth, we find him genuinely concerned on his daughter's account, since he believes that she does not like Darcy. Convinced by her that she does, he comes to like him himself though, like Mrs Bennet, he goes in some awe of him. Typical of his throwaway humour is his remark that he thinks he prefers Wickham to his other future sons-in-law, though we learn later that he enjoys visiting Pemberley unexpectedly, a sure indication that he recognizes the happiness of his daughter and the quality of the man she has married. He is a mixed but convincing character; every now and then seriousness breaks through, but Mr Bennet is essentially a laconic character, having some insight into his own motives, his own selfishness and, sadly, his lack of real sympathetic contact with his wife which he covers by a kind of wit which she often doesn't understand.

Mrs Bennet

The business of her life was to get her daughters married; its solace was visiting and news.

The whole of Chapter 1 is virtually in dialogue, with Mrs Bennet saying much with very little sense. It sets up the pattern by which we judge her. She is a woman of 'mean understanding, little information, and uncertain temper' (Chapter 1, p. 3). This she demonstrates throughout the novel. She has none of the moral sense of her elder daughters. Her account of the ball to Mr Bennet shows how unscrupulous she is – she gives a minute account of all the dancing with an eye to the main chance for Jane, and immediately dislikes Darcy who, of course, has seen her vulgarity displayed. That vulgarity causes her to welcome Lizzie's staying at Netherfield for as long as she can with Jane in order to further by implication Bingley's interest in her eldest daughter. When she visits Netherfield herself she fancies that she has put Darcy down instead of making herself ridiculous.

She tries to delay Elizabeth's and Jane's return from Netherfield, supports Mr Collins's application for Elizabeth's hand in marriage, and contrives to leave her alone with Mr Collins despite her daughter's protestations. On his failure she promises to bring Lizzie to reason, is amazed at the alternative Mr Bennet offers his daughter, and exclaims 'Nobody can tell what I suffer!' (Chapter 20, p. 86).

Her prostration during Lydia's disgrace gives way to undiluted joy when she learns that she is married; earlier she had indulged her melodramatic – and romantic – fears to the full by envisaging a fight between Mr Bennet and Wickham. Before that she has endured the humiliation of Charlotte Lucas's acceptance of Mr Collins, seeing Charlotte as the future mistress of Longbourn. She complains to Mrs Gardiner about Lizzie's perverseness in not accepting Mr Collins. However, her re-emergence into practical activity – if it can ever be called that – from crisis is swift, for she even initially plans which house Lydia could live in in the neighbourhood. Her triumph in having a daughter married at sixteen is loquacious and insensitive, but greater triumphs are to come her way. Bingley's return marks the first, though she contrives to be rude to Darcy. Again she arranges that Bingley and Jane shall be left alone, winking at Kitty and calling Elizabeth away. She is all civility to Lady Catherine when she arrives, little knowing that she has come to castigate her daughter. She apologizes to Elizabeth for leaving her to walk alone with Darcy. After she learns that Elizabeth has accepted him, it is but a moment for her to change her mind about the man she has hitherto found so disagreeable:

What pin-money, what jewels, what carriages you will have! Jane is nothing to it – nothing at all. I am so pleased – so happy! Such a charming man – so handsome! so tall! Oh, my dear Lizzy! pray apologize for my having disliked him so much before. (Chapter 59, p. 281).

This quotation really conveys the essential Mrs Bennet – mercenary, hypocritical, snobbish, having no moral measure but a ready allowance of words which can fit the favourable occasion and show just how shallow she is. Perhaps we laugh at her more than we despise her, but she always puts her own troubles first, and these are for the most part imaginary ones. Measured in terms of her ambitions she achieves what she wants. She is giddy, almost like a girl, and indeed Mr Bennet is witty enough to suggest that Bingley might fancy her instead of one of her daughters. Yet she is not merely caricature, and we note again that Jane Austen is presenting with psychological truth the kind of person who is what she says – there is nothing beneath the surface those words provide.

Lydia

A stout well-grown girl of fifteen, with a fine complexion and good-humoured countenance.

Lydia is brash, silly, unprincipled, given by Jane Austen a family resemblance to her silly mother. She is in pursuit of the officers at Meryton, and at one stage has the effrontery to remind Bingley of his promise to give a ball. She is vulgar and loud, flirtatious and without scruples; in a word, she is superficial, out for what she can get, having no sense of morality, prepared to run away with Wickham even without the promise of marriage. Once she achieves that state, however, she is full of the ostentation and display which has characterized her previous actions – only now it has the stamp of status, enabling her to show off her ring and generally put her sisters down since she has achieved marriage before they have. She is indiscreet, but plays an essential part in the plot, for she reveals to Lizzy that Darcy had been at her wedding. She even usurps Jane's place at table since she is now a married woman. She does her best to get preferment for Wickham via Elizabeth and Darcy, and always has the capacity to cadge and to act without shame.

Kitty

'If *I* should ever go to Brighton, I should behave better than Lydia.'

Kitty is a mirror image for Lydia but, because she is not allowed to follow her taller sister's excesses, she later improves. She is silly and superficial, bitterly jealous when Colonel Forster and his wife invite Lydia to Brighton, and, like her sister, thinks only of officers and clothes. After Lydia's elopement Mr Bennet speaks sternly to her and Kitty fears she will be cut off from an exciting life. At this stage she too has no moral perspective, but by the end of the novel being denied Lydia's company and visiting her elder sisters, Kitty becomes in their superior society 'less irritable, less ignorant, and less insipid' (Chapter 61, p. 286). These are negatives, but they form the basis for change.

Mary

Mary had neither genius nor taste.

Mary is a bore, filled with inflated and pompous statements which have an epigrammatic ring and little substance. She forms an admirable contrast to each of her sisters; where Elizabeth and Jane have cultivated moral perspective and rational judgement, where Lydia and Kitty have indulged the company of officers, Mary is the reader and talker who doesn't fail to pronounce – inadequately – on every situation, whether it be passing incident or family crisis. She piques herself upon 'the solidity of her reflections' (Chapter 5, p. 13) but when she performs after Elizabeth we are told that she had 'a pedantic air and conceited manner' (Chapter 6, p. 17). Darcy provides her with the material for some sententious views on pride and vanity, Lydia's situation with some 'moral extractions' which take the following form:

This is a most unfortunate affair; and will probably be much talked of. But we must stem the tide of malice, and pour into the wounded bosoms of each other the balm of sisterly consolation. (Chapter 47, p. 213).

Jane Austen, as we know, loved many of the great eighteenth century writers, and here in Mary she is parodying the extremes of the weighty rational manner. One almost pities Mrs Bennet and her husband in having so much of Mary after their other three daughters have left home.

Mr Collins

Mr Collins was not a sensible man, and the deficiency of Nature had been but little assisted by education or society.

With the exception of his patroness Lady Catherine de Bourgh, Mr Collins is the outstanding grotesque of *Pride and Prejudice* and, suitably, he echoes the title of the novel at every turn of speech and behaviour. His first letter – and there are to be other equally important ones – conveys the man. To coin Marshall McLuhan's famous phrase, here the medium is the message of the man to come. Pompous, self-important, constantly name-dropping his patroness and her status into his conversation and his letters, the irony with which he is presented shows us Jane Austen at her very best, for here is a Christian clergyman without Christian sentiments.

Intent on marriage in order to satisfy his patroness's wishes, he makes Jane's supposed unavailability the excuse for proposing to Elizabeth, and her rejection the mainspring for his move to Charlotte Lucas. He is a predatory opportunist; he is self-confident and boring, and although he describes his 'present overtures of good-will' as 'highly commendable' (Chapter 13, p. 46), his eye is of course on the Longbourn estates which will one day be his. His conceit and his stupidity are boundless; he considers that Elizabeth's refusal means that she is just behaving after the manner of 'elegant females', for sincerity is beyond his reach. Having used the Bennets he wins Charlotte; having won Charlotte he, admittedly at her wish, shows off Hunsford and Rosings as a charitable way of indicating to Elizabeth what she might have had. He is all deference and subservience to Lady Catherine, having no mind of his own and allowing her to interfere quite freely in his domestic life. But his most Christian effusions are reserved for his letters. After Lydia's elopement he writes to Mr Bennet that 'The death of your daughter would have been a blessing in comparison of this' (Chapter 48, p. 219) and urges him 'to throw off your unworthy child from your affection for ever' (p. 219). An inveterate gossip, he retails the news to Mr Bennet that Elizabeth may shortly marry Darcy and at the same time castigates him for receiving Lydia and Wickham at his home. In short, Mr Collins is a parasite, ridiculous and revolting in his attitude towards the dictatorial Lady Catherine; he has no sense of humour but provides much, particularly in his sycophantic and obsequious attitude towards rank.

Charlotte Collins née Lucas

Charlotte is likeable and drawn with great sensitivity by Jane Austen. She underlines the main theme of *Pride and Prejudice* – the need, economic need apart from anything else for daughters to get married. The reader, like Elizabeth, feels a sense of shock, even of revulsion, when Charlotte marries Mr Collins. She puts practicality before romance and does it honestly, though she blushes for her husband as he shows off their home and fawns on Lady Catherine. There is a quality of pathos in the presentation of Charlotte; she *needs* Elizabeth, hence her encouragement of the visit to Hunsford, because she is trapped. She does not adopt her husband's servility to Lady Catherine, but she is forced to endure the latter's interference. All things considered, she handles her husband well. Aware of his lack of breeding and of his ability to take over conversations, she encourages him to pay some attention to his garden, thus ensuring that she has some relief from his company. It is hardly the basis for a marriage, but Charlotte has gone into it with her eyes open, and her evenness of temper and admirable organization and restraint provide another comment on the nature of marriage itself.

Wickham

. . . the agreeable manner in which he immediately fell into conversation . . .

Handsome, fashionable, easy of manner, persuasive, lacking any moral basis for his actions, Wickham is an ironic comment on the nature of 'first impressions'. His account of his relations with the Darcy family and with Darcy himself is convincing to Elizabeth, for he seems to be what he appears, though later Elizabeth is to question his indiscretion in confiding in her so fully so quickly. A liar and opportunist, Wickham at first appears to pay court to Elizabeth – though perhaps he is merely exercising his talents – then transfers his attentions to the heiress Miss King. Earlier, we are later to learn from Darcy's letter to Elizabeth, he had sought to elope with Georgiana Darcy. Elizabeth is initially charmed by him but no more, yet she accepts what he says unquestioningly and without her usual judgement. Jane of course is loath to believe ill of him. There is little doubt that he only marries Lydia because of Darcy's finding the money to make him comfortable and purchasing a commission in the regulars for him. He is all charm when he and Lydia return married – we should say brazen if he were obtrusive – but is somewhat disconcerted by the fact that Elizabeth knows the truth about him. He is motivated by greed, something which Mr Bennet recognizes in him, and even rather appreciates in his whimsical way this form of roguery in a young man who has made a career by being devious, untruthful, irresponsible and unscrupulous. He and Lydia deserve each other.

Lady Catherine de Bourgh

. . whatever she said, was spoken in so authoritative a tone, as marked her self-importance . . .

The Lady of Rosings is used to power and the constant exercise of it. She has the same kind of dominating presence as the much later Lady Bracknell of Oscar Wilde's *The Importance of Being Earnest* but without any of the humour adhering to that equally formidable and bossy society woman. She lives by status, inflicting her views on all who come within her orbit at Rosings. Her daughter Lady Anne is of a sickly and delicate nature, and there is some pathos in the way Lady Catherine covers this by being jealous of anyone else's accomplishments where her daughter has none. She rules Mr Collins, who is only too glad to be ruled; she pokes about the parsonage at Hunsford and organizes the domestic arrangements there. She is loud, arrogant and obtrusive in company, cherishes the idea that Anne is really betrothed to Darcy by some family arrangement, and receives Elizabeth with the condescension which Mr Collins is so happy to associate with every mention of her name. Her visit to see Elizabeth shows Jane Austen in complete control of character and situation; Elizabeth stands up to her with politeness and spirit, and Lady Catherine, except when she is talking about Anne, has little answer except haughtiness and pride with which to counter the sheer independence and rational armoury which Elizabeth turns upon her. In effect she is defeated by what she is – an inflexible, insensitive, overbearing woman who is incapable of reason. She is rude in company, selfish and indulged in all she does, but in Elizabeth she is faced with integrity and moral perspective, and she loses gracelessly.

Miss Bingley

Miss Bingley began abusing her as soon as she was out of the room.

Miss Bingley is shallow, self-advertising, ill-bred, and has set her own cap at Darcy while propitiating her brother in the direction of Georgiana Darcy. The quotation at the head of this section describes her for what she is: easily jealous of Elizabeth, she talks behind people's backs, condescends to Mrs Bennet and her family (she is of course aware of their vulgarity) and, while affecting to be very fond of Jane has little time for her when

Jane visits London. Darcy sees through her vulgarity; she is always making protestations of sincere interest, but they amount to nothing. Her remarks on Elizabeth's 'fine eyes' lead finally to her being humiliated, particularly at Pemberley where Darcy reveals, under her constant badgering, that he has long considered Elizabeth one of the handsomest women he knows. She is ill-natured, has a natural foil in her sister Mrs Hurst, and seems to have none of her brother's qualities of affability and good humour.

Mr Bingley

A pleasant countenance and easy unaffected manners.

Bingley is easy-going as well as possessing the qualities named above. He is an attractive and engaging young man, and Darcy fears that he will be easily led. In fact there is some evidence of this. His own inclination towards Jane is obvious, and his conduct towards her family is throughout courteous, kindly and considerate. But just as Jane fails to register beside Elizabeth, so Bingley fails to register beside Darcy. He is a foil to the latter, lacking the positive views and attitudes of Darcy, but he compensates by being popular where Darcy is resented or even feared. He is somewhat weak though, to be fair, he is unaware that Jane is in London, having been separated by his family and Darcy from her. His return to Jane at Longbourn is moving and unaffectedly open; if we object to his lack of colour it is because he is seen against Darcy on the one hand and the unscrupulous Wickham on the other.

Other characters

All Jane Austen's minor characters are well done, from the vulgarity of Mrs Philips, who is a gossip and who encourages Lydia and Kitty in their irresponsible ways, to a go-between character like Denny, who is responsible initially for bringing Wickham onto the scene. I do not intend here to go into detail about the minor characters – one could write a brief paragraph on Georgiana Darcy's shyness and inherent goodness, or the pathetic sickliness of Lady Anne – but I think that three of them merit some attention because they subserve the obviously moral context of the novel. I refer to the Gardiners – Darcy nobly withstands their being in trade – and Colonel Fitzwilliam, all of whom exhibit such moral traits as responsibility, concern for others, suitable modesty, intelligence and those qualities of life and living which Jane Austen obviously holds dear. Mrs Gardiner has the good sense to warn Elizabeth about Wickham and, although this is perhaps breaking a confidence, to tell Elizabeth of how much she and her family owe to Darcy in getting Lydia married. She is a woman of sound sense, good manners, and insight – she immediately sees that Darcy is in love with Elizabeth. She contrasts with Mrs Bennet in terms of her considered language and a certain generosity of spirit. Her husband's qualities are perhaps reflected in Darcy's reception of him and his later ability to use his commonsense and practical knowledge in the Lydia affair. He talks sensibly to Elizabeth about it, acts directly and with authority, largely succeeding where Mr Bennet fails. He is a knowledgable man without ostentation; through the Gardiners and their goodness of attitude and action Jane Austen is able to expose the worthless snobbery of rank – as in Lady Catherine – or pretension as, at different levels, in Sir William Lucas and Mr Collins. Sir William is worth a mention if only to illustrate Jane Austen's art of caricature; as subservient as Mr Collins, the words 'St James's' ever-trembling on his lips, his one triumph gives him a talking point for the rest of his life. Colonel Fitzwilliam represents nobility and humility, kindness, consideration, intelligence; he shows some interest in Elizabeth and talks rationally with her. Darcy cites him as a man of integrity to whom Elizabeth may appeal for the truth of his letter. He is another moral lynch-pin in the plot.

Style

General

Students of *Pride and Prejudice* and of Jane Austen's other novels should note the directness, clarity and exactness of her style. She is an economical writer; no words are wasted either in dialogue or commentary. Every sentence moves the narrative forward in terms of situation and action, and one of the reasons why Jane Austen's novels have been so successfully televized, filmed or broadcast on radio is because the lucidity of her language requires very little adjustment. Her writing is natural and un-forced, so that the reader can easily follow what is said. The chapters are generally brief, and this makes for narrative expec-tation. Below I give the main aspects of her style, though the commentaries accompanying the chapter summaries will have given a considered stress to her most common usages.

Dialogue

Jane Austen is the mistress of good, crisp, character-revealing dialogue. A fine example is the first chapter of the novel. Here there are opening and closing statements which offer a brief surround of commentary; the rest of the chapter is in dialogue, dialogue which shows the ambitions and silliness of Mrs Bennet, the wry and somewhat sardonic humour of Mr Bennet. The dialogue also prepares us for the localized dramatic action to come, for the roles in that action to be played by the daughters – who are discussed – and of course by Mr and Mrs Bennet. Miss Bingley's dialogue with Darcy in Chapter 6 reveals her character 'and pray when am I to wish you joy?' (p. 19), but Jane Austen's major ability is to reproduce *society* speech (sometimes over-heard), be it at a ball, an assembly, in the drawing-room at Rosings or at Longbourn. She is very good indeed at capturing the temperature of dialogue in crisis or confrontation, as in Elizabeth's rejection of Darcy and his impassioned response, or, perhaps best of all, in the exchange between Lady Catherine and Elizabeth when Darcy's formidable relation comes to

Longbourn. She is also adept at capturing the dialogue of confidence or revelation, for instance when Wickham tells Elizabeth of Darcy's treatment of him, or when the housekeeper at Pemberley redresses the balance for Darcy by her own informed praise of him. Turns of phrase and speech which define the man or woman are her particular strength; read the spoken words of Mr Collins, Sir William Lucas, Mr Bennet, Mrs Bennet and Lydia, and you would find it impossible to mistake any of these for anyone else in the novel. The dialogue is laced with ironic humour which runs throughout the length of the novel. Again the dialogue contributes to this. Consider Elizabeth's exchange with Darcy, where she picks up his statement and caps it with a related one of her own:

'I have been used to consider poetry as the *food* of love,' said Darcy.
'Of a fine, stout, healthy love it may. – Everything nourishes what is strong already. But if it be only a slight, thin sort of inclination, I am convinced that one good sonnet will starve it entirely away.' (9, 33)

This shows Elizabeth's wit, her ability to improvise, an ability shown in the quality of her conversation.

Commentary

In 19th century fiction the author frequently makes use of his or her own voice to pronounce on the actions or situations of their fictional characters – Thackeray for instance in *Vanity Fair*, George Eliot in *Adam Bede* and Dickens generally, with a particular example from *Bleak House* coming to mind in the splendid personal rhetoric he uses after the death of Jo the crossing-sweeper. Jane Austen opens her novel – and it is one of the most effective and stimulating openings to a novel in English fiction – with the statement:

It is a truth universally acknowledged that a single man in possession of a good fortune must be in want of a wife.

The irony I have mentioned above is present in that statement, since it is not a 'truth' but a conclusion, hope, speculation, whatever you wish. But the author is establishing her mode of telling her story and the statement prepares the reader for the marriage stories which are to come. By the end of the same chapter there is commentary of a specific nature on the characters of Mr and Mrs Bennet. As I have said above, dialogue speaks for Jane Austen through her characters, but there is plenty of commentary on the *consciousness* of those characters and more particularly on the character of Elizabeth, through whose eyes most of the actions are seen. Consider Elizabeth in reaction after Darcy's proposal, or after she has discovered what he has done for her family in the Lydia affair. In *Pride and Prejudice* commentary on inward reaction is balanced by outward description, whether it be of character – Lady Catherine for example – or the description of the walk or of Pemberley in Chapter 43. In a sense, description of this kind is commentary, since it establishes character or background to character.

Letters

Jane Austen inherited the epistolary mode of writing novels from the 18th century, notably from Samuel Richardson, whose novels are written completely in the form of letters. But she adapted it, successfully weaving her letters into the natural narrative of dialogue and description. Often these letters form narrative crisis points or indicate a new direction. Mr Collins's letter announcing his arrival anticipates the role he is to play in the plot; his later letters, about how Mr Bennet should treat Lydia, or his retailing the gossip that Elizabeth will shortly become engaged to Darcy, show Jane Austen using the letter as a plot device. This she does naturally and unobtrusively, with Jane's letters to Elizabeth (at first misdirected) providing information on the Lydia crisis, and Mrs Gardiner's letter to Elizabeth revealing Darcy's part in the arranged wedding of Lydia and Wickham. Perhaps the most important of all is Darcy's letter to Elizabeth which explains his past dealings with Wickham. All these contribute to the movement of the narrative and are, in effect, an echo of the times, for letters were the major means of communication. They provide the drama of expectation; letters are followed by action, whether inward or outward, and they are thus pivotal contributions to the plot.

Humour

Jane Austen is largely a comic writer, and that is in no sense a term of devaluation. The novel is rich in caricature effects, seen for example in Lady Catherine and Mr Collins, both figures of fun, the one grotesque and overbearing, the other ridiculous. Mary is recognizably of the same type, and here the nature of her speech with its loaded and meaningless borrowings which constitute, for her, morality, show the author's ironic conception of character in action. This irony of course plays over Mr and Mrs Bennet and Sir William Lucas too. The wit in the novel belongs largely to Elizabeth, who has a gift for repartee and innuendo which makes her a delightfully spirited creation.

Contrast

Jane Austen makes excellent use of contrast throughout. Consider the character of Darcy (positive), Bingley (somewhat negative) and Wickham (irresponsible, somewhat dissolute) as contrasting types of young men. Elizabeth, Jane and Lydia roughly complement these three. A singular contrast is that between Mr Bennet and Mr Collins, the latter full of words and pomposity, the former sparing of words – though a master of wit – and inaction. The interested student will look closely at the *morality* embodied in the individual characters, for this is an essential part of the intentional contrasting balance.

General questions

1 'Easily the most interesting character in the novel.' Discuss this estimate of Elizabeth in *Pride and Prejudice*.

Note-form guidance for an answer

(a) Most things seen through the eyes of Elizabeth (b) concern for her sister Jane (c) her own spiritedness and independence (d) awareness of her parents' (and other sisters' – not Jane's) shortcomings (e) capable of error (accepts Wickham's account) (f) initial dislike – first impression – of Darcy (g) reaction re Mr Collins's proposal (h) reaction re Charlotte's acceptance of Mr Collins (i) insight into nature of Caroline Bingley (j) standing up to Lady Catherine (at Rosings – preparation for later encounter) (k) rejection of Darcy's proposal (l) goes too far in mentioning Wickham's grievance (m) taxes him with spoiling Jane's happiness (n) gradually changes feelings after receiving Darcy's letter.

THEN trace Elizabeth's discoveries, changes, love.

Look across at any other characters (briefly) and say if they command the interest which Elizabeth does (and why if they do).

CONCLUSION brief paragraph based on individual judgement of interest/importance of Elizabeth.

2 'Nothing much happens.' Is this an accurate account of the plot and action of *Pride and Prejudice*?

3 Write an essay on Jane Austen's use of letters and their effects in *Pride and Prejudice*.

4 Compare and contrast Wickham and Bingley.

5 In what ways do you find Mr Collins (a) grotesque and (b) unchristian? You should refer closely to the text in your answer.

6 Analyse a section of dialogue from any *two* chapters, saying what it reveals of the characters concerned.

7 '*Pride and Prejudice* is about money and marriage.' How far would you agree with this statement?

8 Compare and contrast Lady Catherine de Bourgh and Mrs Bennet.

9 In what ways do you find Mr Bennet an unsympathetic character?

10 Compare and contrast Lydia and Charlotte Lucas later Collins.

11 In what ways do you think that *First Impressions* was a suitable title for the novel?

12 What **do** you consider to be the most dramatic incident in the novel? Give reasons for your choice.

13 Write an essay on the variety of Jane Austen's humour in *Pride and Prejudice*.

14 What qualities do you most (a) admire and (b) dislike in the character of Darcy?

15 'It is an exposure of moral irresponsibility.' How far is this a true estimate of the nature of *Pride and Prejudice*?

16 In what ways does jealousy play an important part in *Pride and Prejudice*?

17 In what ways do Mr and Mrs Gardiner contribute to the action of *Pride and Prejudice*?

18 Compare the attitudes of Elizabeth and Jane to the various events in the novel.

19 Write about any *three* minor characters not mentioned above.

20 Write an essay on what you find most interesting in *Pride and Prejudice*.

Further reading

Other novels by Jane Austen (all available in Pan Books)
Sense and Sensibility
Persuasion
Mansfield Park
Emma
Jane Austen and Her World, Marghanita Laski (Thames and Hudson).
Critical Essays on Jane Austen, ed. Brian Southam (Routledge and Kegan Paul).
A Reading of Jane Austen, Barbara Hardy (Athlone Press).
Jane Austen and Her Art, Mary Lascelles (Oxford University Press).

Pan study aids Titles published in the Brodie's Notes series

W. H. Auden Selected Poetry

Jane Austen Emma Mansfield Park Northanger Abbey Persuasion
Pride and Prejudice

Anthologies of Poetry Ten Twentieth Century Poets The Poet's Tale
The Metaphysical Poets

Samuel Beckett Waiting for Godot

Arnold Bennett The Old Wives' Tale

William Blake Songs of Innocence and Experience

Robert Bolt A Man for All Seasons

Harold Brighouse Hobson's Choice

Charlotte Brontë Jane Eyre

Emily Brontë Wuthering Heights

Robert Browning Selected Poetry

John Bunyan The Pilgrim's Progress

Geoffrey Chaucer (parallel texts editions) The Franklin's Tale
The Knight's Tale The Miller's Tale The Nun's Priest's Tale
The Pardoner's Tale Prologue to the Canterbury Tales
The Wife of Bath's Tale

Richard Church Over the Bridge

John Clare Selected Poetry and Prose

Samuel Taylor Coleridge Selected Poetry and Prose

Wilkie Collins The Woman in White

William Congreve The Way of the World

Joseph Conrad The Nigger of the Narcissus & Youth
The Secret Agent

Charles Dickens Bleak House David Copperfield Dombey and Son
Great Expectations Hard Times Little Dorrit Oliver Twist
Our Mutual Friend A Tale of Two Cities

Gerald Durrell My Family and Other Animals

George Eliot Middlemarch The Mill on the Floss Silas Marner

T. S. Eliot Murder in the Cathedral Selected Poems

J. G. Farrell The Siege of Krishnapur

Henry Fielding Joseph Andrews

F. Scott Fitzgerald The Great Gatsby

E. M. Forster Howards End A Passage to India
Where Angels Fear to Tread

William Golding Lord of the Flies The Spire

Oliver Goldsmith Two Plays of Goldsmith: She Stoops to Conquer;
The Good Natured Man

Graham Greene Brighton Rock The Power and the Glory
The Quiet American

Thom Gunn and Ted Hughes Selected Poems

Thomas Hardy Chosen Poems of Thomas Hardy
Far from the Madding Crowd Jude the Obscure
The Mayor of Casterbridge Return of the Native
Tess of the d'Urbervilles The Trumpet-Major

L. P. Hartley The Go-Between The Shrimp and the Anemone

Joseph Heller Catch-22

Ernest Hemingway For Whom the Bell Tolls
The Old Man and the Sea

Barry Hines A Kestrel for a Knave

Gerard Manley Hopkins Poetry and Prose of Gerard Manley Hopkins

Aldous Huxley Brave New World

Henry James Washington Square

Ben Jonson The Alchemist Volpone

James Joyce A Portrait of the Artist as a Young Man

John Keats Selected Poems and Letters of John Keats

Ken Kesey One Flew over the Cuckoo's Nest

Rudyard Kipling Kim

D. H. Lawrence The Rainbow Selected Tales Sons and Lovers

Harper Lee To Kill a Mockingbird

Laurie Lee As I Walked out One Midsummer Morning
Cider with Rosie

Thomas Mann Death in Venice & Tonio Kröger

Christopher Marlowe Doctor Faustus Edward the Second

W. Somerset Maugham Of Human Bondage

Gavin Maxwell Ring of Bright Water

Arthur Miller The Crucible Death of a Salesman

John Milton A Choice of Milton's Verse Comus and Samson
Agonistes Paradise Lost I, II

Sean O'Casey Juno and the Paycock
The Shadow of a Gunman and the Plough and the Stars

George Orwell Animal Farm 1984

John Osborne Luther

Alexander Pope Selected Poetry

J. B. Priestley An Inspector Calls

Siegfried Sassoon Memoirs of a Fox-Hunting Man

Peter Shaffer The Royal Hunt of the Sun

William Shakespeare Antony and Cleopatra As You Like It
Coriolanus Hamlet Henry IV (Part 1) Henry IV (Part 2) Henry V
Julius Caesar King Lear Love's Labour's Lost Macbeth Measure for
Measure The Merchant of Venice A Midsummer Night's Dream
Much Ado about Nothing Othello Richard II Richard III Romeo and
Juliet The Sonnets The Taming of the Shrew The Tempest Twelfth
Night The Winter's Tale

G. B. Shaw Androcles and the Lion Arms and the Man
Caesar and Cleopatra The Doctor's Dilemma Pygmalion Saint Joan

Richard Sheridan Plays of Sheridan: The Rivals; The Critic;
The School for Scandal

John Steinbeck The Grapes of Wrath Of Mice and Men & The Pearl

Tom Stoppard Rosencrantz and Guildenstern are Dead

J. M. Synge The Playboy of the Western World

Jonathan Swift Gulliver's Travels

Alfred Tennyson Selected Poetry

William Thackeray Vanity Fair

Flora Thompson Lark Rise to Candleford

Dylan Thomas Under Milk Wood

Anthony Trollope Barchester Towers

Mark Twain Huckleberry Finn

Keith Waterhouse Billy Liar

Evelyn Waugh Decline and Fall Scoop

H. G. Wells The History of Mr Polly The War of the Worlds

John Webster The White Devil

Oscar Wilde The Importance of Being Earnest

Virginia Woolf To the Lighthouse

William Wordsworth The Prelude (Books 1, 2)

John Wyndham The Chrysalids

W. B. Yeats Selected Poetry

Pan study aids

Published jointly by Heinemann Educational Books and Pan Books

Pan Study Aids is a major new series developed to help school and college students prepare for examinations. All the authors are experienced teachers/examiners at O level, School Certificate and equivalent examinations and authors of textbooks used in schools and colleges worldwide

Each volume in the series:

- explains its subject and covers clearly and concisely and with excellent illustrations the essential points of the syllabus, drawing attention to common areas of difficulty and to areas which carry most marks in the exam

- gives guidance on how to plan revision, and prepare for the exam, outlining what examiners are looking for

- provides practice by including typical exam questions and exercises

Titles available: Physics, Chemistry, Maths, Human Biology, English Language, Geography 1 & 2, Economics, Commerce, Accounts and Book-keeping, British Government and Politics, History 1 & 2, Effective Study Skills, French, German, Spanish, Sociology